# LECTIN FREE COOKBOOK

How to Kick-start the Lectin-free Diet and Potential Risks

(Want to Have a Healthy Diet by Choosing a Safe Food?)

**Dannielle Hoppe**

Published by Alex Howard

© **Dannielle Hoppe**

All Rights Reserved

*Lectin Free Cookbook: How to Kick-start the Lectin-free Diet and Potential Risks (Want to Have a Healthy Diet by Choosing a Safe Food?)*

**ISBN 978-1-990169-18-2**

All rights reserved. No part of this guide may be reproduced in any form without permission in writing from the publisher except in the case of brief quotations embodied in critical articles or reviews.

**Legal & Disclaimer**

The information contained in this book is not designed to replace or take the place of any form of medicine or professional medical advice. The information in this book has been provided for educational and entertainment purposes only.

The information contained in this book has been compiled from sources deemed reliable, and it is accurate to the best of the Author's knowledge; however, the Author cannot guarantee its accuracy and validity and cannot be held liable for any errors or omissions. Changes are periodically made to this book. You must consult your doctor or get professional medical advice before using any of the suggested remedies, techniques, or information in this book.

# Table of contents

**PART 1** ............................................................................................... 1

**INTRODUCTION** ................................................................................ 2

**CHAPTER 1: WHAT IS THE DEFINITION OF LECTIN?** ......................... 4

What Is The Lectin-Free Diet? .............................................................. 4
Why Are Lectins So Crucial? ................................................................. 5
What You Should Think About Lectins ................................................. 6
Products Of The Soil That Contain Lectins Are: .................................... 8
Potential Advantages Of Plant Sustenance Lectins .............................. 9
Devouring A Lot Of Lectins Can Be Detrimental ................................ 10
Overexposure To Lectins Can Trigger Autoimmune Disease ............. 12
You Can Remove Lectins By Cooking Your Food ................................ 12
Douse, Sprout And Ferment Legumes To Make Them Safer ............. 13
Lectins In Canned Legumes ................................................................ 14
Lectins, Agglutinins, And Their Parts In Immune System Reactivities ................ 15

**CHAPTER 2: HOW WOULD YOU STAY AWAY FROM LECTINS?** ....... 16

Fact About 6 Foods That Are High In Lectins ..................................... 19
Red Kidney Beans ............................................................................... 19
Soybeans ............................................................................................ 21
Peanuts .............................................................................................. 22
Tomatoes ........................................................................................... 23
Potatoes ............................................................................................ 24

**CHAPTER 3: MANAGING LECTINS** ................................................. 25

All That You Need To Know ................................................................ 27
Where Do They Come From? ............................................................. 27
Eating Routine Without The Die ........................................................ 28
I. Health Risks Of Being Overweight ................................................... 28
Gallstones (In Ladies) ......................................................................... 29
Memory And Learning Problems (In Men) ........................................ 29
II. Psychological Consequences Of Being Overweight ....................... 30
III. Loss Of Energy And Joy For Life ..................................................... 31

Sam From Oakland, Dc .................................................................. 32
Lizzy From Los Angeles ................................................................ 34

## CHAPTER 4: WHY DO WE GAIN WEIGHT? .................................................... 35

1. Your Thyroid Is Sluggish ......................................................... 36
2. You Overeat Healthy Foods ........................................................ 37
3. You're Dehydrated ................................................................ 37
4. You're Depressed ................................................................. 38
5. You Avoid The Scale .............................................................. 38
6. You're Obsessed With Spinning .................................................... 39
7. You Don't Check Yourself Out ..................................................... 39
8. You Stay Up Late ................................................................. 40
9. Your Job Is Really Stressful ..................................................... 40
10. You Don't Eat Enough Protein .................................................... 41
11. You Never Indulge ............................................................... 41
12. You're Taking Medication ........................................................ 42

## CHAPTER 5: NUTRITION AND WEIGHT LOSS .................................................. 43

Habits That Can Help You Lose Weight ................................................ 46

## CHAPTER 6: LECTIN-FREE VEGAN AND NON-VEGAN RECIPES .................................... 48

1. Sweet Potato Hash ................................................................ 48
2. Homemade Granola Bars (Grain-Free, Lectin-Free) .................................. 50

## 3. LECTIN-FREE VEGAN TACO "MEAT" ...................................................... 52

4. Cinnamon Cassava Flour Pancakes .................................................. 53
5. Cilantro Lime Salmon Burgers {Paleo, Gluten-Free & Lectin-Free} .................. 55
6. Tasty Chewy Gingerbread In A Mug ................................................. 57
7. Lectin-Free Vegan Shirataki Angel Hair Pasta With Creamy Chipotle Avocado Sauce ............................................................................. 59
8. Lectin-Free Cesar Salad .......................................................... 61
9. Lectin Free Pasta Recipe ......................................................... 63
10. Grilled Sirloin Steak And Leeks With Arugula-Oregano Dressing ................... 65
11. Tempeh Bacon (Gluten-Free, Lectin-Free) ......................................... 67
12. Large Cassava Tortillas (Grain-Free, Vegan, & Lectin-Free) ...................... 69
13. Roasted Cauliflower Rice ........................................................ 71

14. Stir Fry Broccoli Cooked In Teriyaki Sauce Served With Cauliflower Rice (Vegan, Lectin-Free & Sugar-Free) .................. 73
15. Lectin-Free Vegan Pumpkin Spice Cauliflower Rice Soup ............ 75

## CONCLUSION .................................................................... 77

## PART 2 ............................................................................... 79

## INTRODUCTION ................................................................. 80

## CHAPTER 1: NUTRIENT ABSORPTION ............................. 82

## CHAPTER 2: METHODS TO REDUCE LECTIN CONTENT ............................. 84

## CHAPTER 3: BENEFITS AND POSSIBLE RISKS OF LECTIN-FREE DIET ............. 87

## CHAPTER 4: BASIC HEALTHY EATING GUIDELINES ............................. 89

## CHAPTER 5: ADVANTAGES OF USING AN INSTANT POT ELECTRIC PRESSURE COOKER ............................................................................ 91

## CHAPTER 6: BREAKFAST RECIPES ................................... 93

## HARD BOILED EGGS ............................................................ 93

Egg Muffins .......................................................................... 95
Crust Free Broccoli And Ham Quiche ................................... 96
Vanilla Muffin ....................................................................... 97
Glory Muffins ........................................................................ 99
Picatta Potatoes ................................................................... 101
Ginger Bread ....................................................................... 102
Almond Flour Biscuits ......................................................... 104
Early Morning Artichokes ................................................... 106

## CHAPTER 7: MAIN DISHES ................................................ 107

Salmon Cakes ....................................................................... 107
Cucumber Salmon Bites ....................................................... 109
Salmon Bowls Asian Style .................................................... 110
Flavour Bomb Asian Brussels Sprouts ................................ 112
Shrimps On Lettuce Leaves ................................................. 114
Amazingly Adaptable Roasted Sweet Potatoes .................. 116
Southern Stewed Greens ..................................................... 117
Balsamic And Garlic Stewed Kale ....................................... 119

Shrimp Tacos With Pomegranate Salsa ........................................................................ 120
Salmon Salad With Avocado Salsa ............................................................................... 122
Cod With Citrus And Fennel Salad ............................................................................... 124
Perfect Cauliflower Mash ............................................................................................ 126
Chicken And Goat Cheese Enchiladas ......................................................................... 127
Steamed Cod With Herbs And Lemon ........................................................................ 129
10-Minute Balsamic Roasted Beets ............................................................................. 130
Garlicky Mashed Sweet Potatoes ................................................................................ 131
Easiest Baked Sweet Potatoes .................................................................................... 133
Herb Roasted Whole Chicken ..................................................................................... 134
Tacos With Ham .......................................................................................................... 136
Fettuccine Alfredo ....................................................................................................... 138
Simplest Brothy Beans ................................................................................................ 140
Chicken Tortellini ........................................................................................................ 141
Chicken Cease ............................................................................................................. 143
Chicken And Spinach Quiche ...................................................................................... 144
Quail Tortellini ............................................................................................................. 145
Beef Stroganoff With Miracle Noodles ....................................................................... 147
Burrito With Pork ........................................................................................................ 149
Meat Lovers Quiche .................................................................................................... 151
Beef Inventory ............................................................................................................. 152
Braised Pork With Italian Seasoning ........................................................................... 153
Tacos With Bacon ........................................................................................................ 154
Stuffed Bacon In Artichoke ......................................................................................... 156
Lamb With Portobello Mushrooms ............................................................................. 157
Ham Filled Egg Muffins ............................................................................................... 158
Cabbage Rolls With Pork ............................................................................................. 159
Braised Pork With Marinara Sauce ............................................................................. 161
Fiery BBQ Meat Balls ................................................................................................... 162
Lamb Empanadas ........................................................................................................ 163
Pork With Risotto ........................................................................................................ 165

**CHAPTER 8: SNACKS** ................................................................................................ 166

Pressure Cooked Onion With Herbed Butter .............................................................. 166
Pressure Cooker Polenta ............................................................................................. 168
Steamed Sweet Potatoes ............................................................................................ 169

Caramelized Onion .................................................................................. 170
Roasted Whole Garlic ............................................................................ 171
Roasted Whole Garlic With Herded Butter .................................................. 172

## CHAPTER 9: SOUPS AND SALADS ........................................................ 173

Easy Noodle Soup .................................................................................. 173
Caesar Salads ....................................................................................... 175
Cauliflower Soup ................................................................................... 177
Asparagus Salad ................................................................................... 179
Smoked Paprika Lentil Soup .................................................................... 181
Orzo Soup With Butternut Squash ............................................................ 183
Fall Kale Salad ...................................................................................... 185
Mixed Veggie Soup ................................................................................ 187
Seed-Sar Salad ..................................................................................... 189
Broccoli Cheddar Soup ........................................................................... 191

# Part 1

# Introduction

**HOW TO KICK-START THE LECTIN FREE DIET**

What do you think about when you hear the expression, sound nourishments? I know...I know you consider bland steamed broccoli and dry chicken with no taste. You get that feared mental picture of frightful bland nourishments that make you would prefer even not to eat any longer. Well uplifting news I'm here to disclose to you that your rundown of solid eating regimen sustenances does not need to be dull and boring!

There are numerous nourishment's that you can eat that are both nutritious and taste well. Doubtlessly the sustenance's that you eat all the time that you believe are undesirable can be made into something that is nutritious and also great tasting. Some of the time it just takes a little creative energy. Did you realize that you can make spaghetti and meatballs into an extraordinary tasting sound dinner? Simply substitute the normal pasta for entire wheat, the ground hamburger for ground turkey and viola! You have a sound supper there sitting tight for you.

I for one adore pasta so I do this with huge numbers of my pasta dinners. For chicken I utilize chicken bosom, for anything that calls for ground meat I utilize turkey rather and obviously I just purchase entire wheat pasta. I just utilize Avocado oil in my cooking which gives great and healthy fat rather than jus FAT contained in different oils. So now and again individuals see me ADDING avocado oil to my seared chicken bosom and ponder what on the planet am I doing in case I should be on an "eating regimen."

A few things are difficult to make solid, for example, meats with high fat substance, and you should attempt to confine sugar however much as could reasonably be expected. Be that as it may, the thing is that it's OK to have these things sometimes. You don't need to eat similar things nonstop for whatever remains of your life. It's OK to carry on a bit, saying this, now I invite you to read this book, to take a look of this trend diet, and be finally aware about the benefits and what they do not want you to know about it! But first, what is exactly Lectin?

# Chapter 1: What Is The Definition Of Lectin?

Lectin's are bounteous in crude vegetables and grains, and most ordinarily found in the piece of the seed that turns into the leaves when the plant grows, otherwise known as the cotyledon, yet additionally on the seed coat. They're likewise found in dairy items and certain vegetables. While lectin content in nourishment is genuinely consistent, the hereditary adjusting of plants has made a few variances.

Lectins are a kind of protein that, in people, may enable cells to connect with each other. A few researchers additionally trust that lectins give a type of resistance in plants to fend off bugs. These proteins likewise contain nitrogen, which is required for plants to develop. While numerous parts of plants contain lectins, the seed is the part that individuals eat regularly.

Lectins may affect wellbeing in different routes, extending from absorption to perpetual sickness chance. They have been appeared to make red platelets group together.

They are classified as antinutrients since they hinder the assimilation of a few supplements.

## What Is The Lectin-Free Diet?

The without lectin eating routine takes out high lectin nourishments like grains, quinoa, vegetables, and nightshade vegetables like tomatoes, peppers, and eggplant and furthermore on the don't eat list: dairy, out-of-season organic product, and expectedly raised meat and poultry. Womp, womp. Rather, the eating regimen proposes you stack your plate with low-lectin sustenances like verdant greens, veggies like cauliflower, broccoli, and asparagus, mushrooms, nuts and seeds, millet, field raised meats, and wild-got angle.

## Why Are Lectins So Crucial?

Lectins are thought to assume a part in insusceptible capacity, cell development, cell demise, and muscle to fat ratio direction.

### INSUSCEPTIBLE REACTION AND POISONOUS QUALITY

Since we don't process lectins, we frequently deliver antibodies to them. Nearly everybody has antibodies to some dietary lectins in their body. This implies our reactions differ. Certain nourishments can even wind up terrible to somebody after an invulnerable framework change or the gut is harmed from another source. The nearness of specific lectins can animate an insusceptible framework reaction. There are a few lectins that nobody ought to expend. Ever ask why you don't see grew red kidney beans?

It's expected to phytohaemagglutinin – a lectin that can cause red kidney bean harming. The harming is typically caused by the ingestion of crude, drenched kidney beans. As few as four or five crude beans can trigger side effects.

Crude kidney beans contain from 20,000 to 70,000 lectin units, while completely cooked beans for the most part contain in the vicinity of 200 and 400 units.

### VALUABLE LECTINS

While numerous kinds of lectins cause negative responses in the body, there are likewise wellbeing advancing lectins that can diminish rate of specific illnesses. Moreover, the body utilizes lectins to accomplish numerous fundamental capacities, including cell to cell adherence, incendiary balance and modified cell passing.

## What You Should Think About Lectins

Ingesting lectins can cause tooting. Expending vegetables and grains in their crude frame can even outcome in queasiness, the runs and regurgitating. For sure, specialists theorize that numerous evident reasons for bacterial sustenance harming may really be lectin harming.

**Risk**

The without lectin eating regimen is a prohibitive arrangement, which may make it troublesome for a few people to tail it long haul.

The arrangement additionally points of confinement or removes numerous nutritious nourishments, for example, entire grains, beans, and certain vegetables. Research has demonstrated that devouring entire grains can help lessen the hazard for coronary illness, diabetes, and growth. Foods grown from the ground likewise have numerous related medical advantages.

Eating more foods grown from the ground may bring down the hazard for numerous conditions, including heart and lung ailments. They may likewise affect disease hazard and help individuals abstain from putting on weight.

A sans lectin eating regimen might be troublesome for veggie lovers or vegetarians to take after, since vegetables, nuts, seeds, and entire grains give plant-based protein.

Vegetables, entire grains, and foods grown from the ground peels likewise give dietary fiber. A sans lectin eating regimen could bring about stoppage if dietary fiber consumption diminishes.

Additionally, following a without lectin eating routine might be costly, as the arrangement prescribes strength milks, field raised meats, and costly supplements.

Now that you have the knowledge and the definition of Lectin let's check some of the most common Lectin nourishments

## Products Of The Soil That Contain Lectins Are:
- Beans
- Carrots
- Cherries
- Grape
- Raspberries
- Blackberries
- Pomegranates
- Cantaloupe
- Lentil sprout,soyabean mung bean
- Green peas
- Zucchini
- Peanuts

Key point: Lectins are proteins that objective and tie sugars.

They are found in numerous sustenance's, however they are more packed in grains and vegetables.

### WOULD IT BE A GOOD IDEA FOR YOU TO DUMP LECTIN?

While going without lectin may encourage a few people, it likely won't fathom everybody's stomach issues. "It's not something or other that ought to be connected all around," says Goodson. "In case you're having significant issues, converse with your specialist or see an enrolled dietitian."

Additionally, just 10 percent of Americans get the suggested day by day measure of products of the soil, says Goodson, so we ought to eat more, not less deliver. "In the event that you take a gander at the advantages of organic products, vegetables, and entire grains for heart wellbeing and bringing down sickness hazard, I will contend that a smidgen of foods grown from the ground will help individuals versus hurt them.

## Potential Advantages Of Plant Sustenance Lectins

Plant lectins tie starches amid processing, moderating or keeping their breakdown, and accordingly decreasing the glycemic impacts of the food.You may hear a claim that lectins "upset absorption," yet this is misdirecting.

This activity of lectins is in all probability a contributing element to the master weight reduction and hostile to diabetes impacts of beans and other plant sustenances.

Beans are wealthy in hostile to growth phytochemicals and are the nourishments exhibiting the most ground-breaking relationship with bring down rates of bosom tumor in enormous epidemiological investigations, including the Nurses' Health Study.

A lectin in like manner mushrooms has been found to restrain multiplication of growth cells in vitro. Mushrooms are another sustenance offering great security against cancer.And that is not by any means the only one: comparative outcomes have been found for lectins from fava beans, soybeans, bananas, buckwheat, jackfruit, and wheat.Some of these lectins are being examined as potential growth therapies.Certain plant nourishment lectins may likewise help forestall tumor improvement by hindering the activities of angiogenesis-advancing lectins on human cells.

**FOODS TO EAT**
- A2 milk
- Cooked sweet potatoes
- Celery
- Avocado

- Mushrooms
- Garlic and onion
- Asparagus
- Cruciferous vegetables
- Olives or extra virgin olive oil
- Leafy, green vegetables
- Pasture-raised meats

**FOODS TO AVOID**

individuals should constrain the accompanying nourishments when attempting to keep away from lectins:

- Squash
- Legumes, such as beans, peas, lentils and peanuts
- Nightshade vegetables, such as eggplant, peppers, potatoes and tomatoes
- Grains
- Fruit, although in-season fruit is allowed in moderation
- Corn
- Meat from corn-fed animals
- A1 milk

## Devouring A Lot Of Lectins Can Be Detrimental

People don't have the best possible proteins important to process lectins.

As they go through the stomach, lectins remain to a great extent unaltered.

When they achieve the digestion tracts, they can connect to the coating of the gut.

In one examination that was led on rodents, lectins endured the stomach and appended themselves to the small digestion tracts. They incidentally thickened the dividers of the small digestion tracts, influencing their capacity to assimilate supplements.

They likewise changed the length and capacity of the whole stomach related tract.

These impacts were for the most part endless supply of lectin from the eating routine.

Lectins can improve pancreas development and increment the arrival of stomach related chemicals.

Lectins make it troublesome for the body to keep up its own particular cells.

Thusly, individuals with harm from lectins may encounter more stomach related issues. This may happen step by step.

Phytohaemagglutinin are the most normally examined lectins. Kidney beans are one of the fundamental wellsprings of these proteins.

On the off chance that you eat crude kidney beans, you can encounter real torment in your stomach area, the runs and regurgitating.

These are side effects of lectin harmfulness .

Indeed, one clinic offered free nourishment to clients amid a "good dieting day" in 1988.

Eleven of the clients who had eaten an extensive number of kidney beans experienced extraordinary stomach related trouble that day.

Be that as it may, you're not prone to eat crude kidney beans.

In the event that you buy canned beans, they have been splashed and cooked before canning.

Dried beans must be arranged appropriately to crush a large number of the lectins.

An excessive amount of Dietary Lectins Can Cause Leaky Gut

The gut divider winds up harmed when lectins join to it.

The modest hairs that line the mucosa wind up harmed and turn out to be less ready to extricate supplements from nourishment.

In an ordinary intestinal covering, the phones are firmly stuffed. They frame what is alluded to as "tight intersections."

This keeps undesirable substances and particles from spilling through the intestinal dividers and entering the circulatory system.

These intestinal cells and their tight intersections are exceptionally connected to invulnerable procedures.

When they are imperiled, resistant reactions to antigens change. As lectins enter the circulation system through the now-penetrable intestinal divider, they join to glycoproteins outwardly of cells.

## Overexposure To Lectins Can Trigger Autoimmune Disease

Lectins may also target antibodies, which help fight disease. In reaction, the immune system attacks the cells.

If the lectins are bound within the tissues of the body, the body may attack itself.

Wheat gliadin is a lectin that causes celiac disease.

It is often referred to as the "celiac disease toxin".

People who are sensitive to this lectin may have a deficiency in certain peptides and a deficiency in their immune systems.

The autoimmune disease diabetes mellitus is linked to the lectin found in tomatoes.

Researchers have found connections between lectins and rheumatoid arthritis as well.

Key point: Albeit immune system illnesses are associated with lacks some place in the invulnerable framework, a few analysts trust that they are caused or exacerbated by specific lectins.

## You Can Remove Lectins By Cooking Your Food

Followers of the Paleo diet typically don't eat legumes because they contain lectins.

Although proper preparation methods can reduce or eliminate lectins in certain foods, if you don't know how the food was cooked, you may want to avoid it.

However, legumes contain carbohydrates, fiber and protein, and they can be very nutritious.

Research shows that simply soaking and boiling legumes for adequate amounts of time can remove virtually all of the lectins.

If you don't soak your beans long enough, you may not be able to encourage the heat to penetrate deeply enough to destroy all of the toxins.

You can't just bake beans under dry heat, either. Research shows that dry heat doesn't inactivate the lectins like boiling does.

In addition, low temperatures can actually increase lectin activity. This is why a slow cooker may not be the ideal vessel for cooking beans.

The amount of hemagglutinating units in raw red kidney beans is between 20,000 and 70,000 hau.

After cooking them properly, red kidney beans only contain about 200 to 400 hau.

Some research has shown that soybeans only need to be boiled for 5 to 10 minutes to eliminate almost all lectin activity.

## Douse, Sprout And Ferment Legumes To Make Them Safer

The two lectins and phytates hinder your body's retention of supplements.

Albeit bubbling under huge warmth can lessen lectins in nourishment, you can decrease the lectin action without warm treatment.

Splashing seeds and grains previously enabling them to grow, or grow, can help lessen lectins and phytates.

In any case, be watchful when you grow vegetables.

Growing certain sorts of seeds or vegetables, similar to lentils and horse feed, can really expand their lectin action.

In the event that you mature seeds and grains, you are basically enabling gainful microbes to eat the lectins.

This can lessen lectin action in sustenances, making them less demanding on the stomach related framework.

Albeit these days most grains are handled in sustenance producing offices, grains were customarily aged before utilization.

## Lectins In Canned Legumes

Normally canned vegetables experience these stages: cleaning, hydration, electronic or manual arrangement post hydration, whitening, bundling, expansion of sauce or brackish water, seaming of the jars, warm handling, solidifying, and naming.

What we are worried about is the whitening, and the warm handling as these can deactivate the lectins.

Ordinarily the warming treatment (in high temp water) amid the canning procedure is sufficient to deactivate the lectins.

In any case, if you are uncertain you can contact the maker of canned vegetables about their warming procedure.

Key point: Canned vegetables ordinarily have their lectins pulverized amid the warming treatment of the canning procedure.

## Lectins, Agglutinins, And Their Parts In Immune System Reactivities

Lectins are starch restricting proteins exhibit all through nature that go about as agglutinins. Roughly 30% of our sustenance contains lectins, some of which might be sufficiently safe to processing to enter the course. As a result of their coupling properties, lectins can cause supplement inadequacies, upset assimilation, and cause extreme intestinal harm when devoured in abundance by a person with broken proteins. These impacts are trailed by interruption of intestinal boundary respectability, which is the door to different autoimmunities. Shared amino corrosive themes between dietary lectins, exogenous peptides, and different body tissues may prompt cross-reactivity, bringing about the generation of antibodies against lectin and bacterial antigens, trailed via autoimmunity. The location of immunoglobulin G (IgG) or immunoglobulin An (IgA) antibodies against particular lectins may fill in as a guide for the end of these lectins from the eating regimen. It is suggested that this procedure can diminish the fringe antigenic boost and, subsequently, result in a lessening of illness indications in a few however not all-patients with immune system issue.

# Chapter 2: How Would You Stay Away From Lectins?

You needed to attempt ,without lectin abstain from food, you'd evade the sustenances that contain them. These include:
Beans and vegetables, including soy and peanuts
Grains
Nightshade vegetables like tomatoes, eggplant, potatoes, and peppers
Bovine's drain and eggs (since dairy cows and business chickens are bolstered lectin-containing grains like wheat and corn)
Obviously, you'd likewise need to avoid any prepared or bundled sustenances that contain these fixings. Some of the time they're self-evident—like on account of jostled tomato sauce or canned dark bean soup. However, some of the time they're tricky. There may be a soy-based thickener in your locally acquired plate of mixed greens dressing or a corn-based sweetener in your breakfast oat, for example.

**WOULD IT BE A GOOD IDEA FOR YOU TO TAKE A STAB AT GOING WITHOUT LECTIN?**

All things considered, it won't hurt you. Be that as it may, it presumably won't benefit you in any way, either, say Palumbo and Meyer. In addition to the fact that it would be extremely troublesome—there's horrible confirmation demonstrating that you may profit. "These fearmongers who need to offer books, they're scoundrels," Palumbo says. "They're searching for that small something that they can blow up into a sensational claim. It's taking a tad of right data, yet it's not the entire story."
In addition, there's a decent possibility that you'd pass up a great opportunity for some vital supplements. Entire grains, beans, and vegetables are rich wellsprings of fiber, which is all

around perceived as critical for keeping up a sound weight, bringing down the hazard for coronary illness, and advancing solid glucose levels. "So the exploration focuses to the opposite, Meyer says. "These nourishments encourage us, they don't hurt." The one exemption? On the off chance that you battle with stomach related issues and haven't discovered alleviation by killing different nourishments (like gluten or FODMAPs), there's no damage in observing in the case of disposing of lectins may help,sayings. Simply make a point to work with an enlisted dietitian, ideally one who has practical experience in stomach related problems. She can supervise your eating regimen to guarantee that you're wiping out nourishments in the correct way and that regardless you'll get all the sustenance you require.

## CAN LECTIN FREE DIET ACTUALLY HELP YOU LOSE WEIGHT?

Lossing 70 beats on a sans lectin abstain from food, and that is as put numerous on patients on this arrangement also. "The astounding thing is when individuals change nothing aside from evacuating significant lectins, they begin getting more fit despite everything they are eating bunches of calories, however we're not putting away it as fat any longer,". A sans lectin eating regimen can positively affect individuals with cardiovascular illness and metabolic disorder (a gathering of conditions showed by expanded circulatory strain, high glucose levels, abundance muscle versus fat around the midsection, and unusual cholesterol levels).

In any case, different specialists are doubtful about how successful it is. "Whenever an eating routine begins to take out a huge measure of nutritional categories, it's somewhat more faddish by nature," says Goodson. "The advantages of eating entire grains and vegetables, which give vitamins, minerals, and fiber, altogether exceed the hazard that a little measure of lectin will cause GI issues."

"We ought to eat more, not less deliver."

Furthermore, most subtenances with lectins can be super useful for weight reduction, says Samantha Cassetty, R.D. For instance, one 2017 examination distributed in the American Journal of Clinical Nutrition connected entire grains with weight reduction.

Furthermore, another investigation distributed in a similar diary found that individuals who devoured beats over a six-week time span (a.k.a. beans, lentils, chickpeas) lost essentially more weight than the individuals who didn't devour any heartbeats.

Be that as it may, Leah Kaufman, R.D., has seen weight reduction achievement in patients with IBS through disposing of certain lectin-containing sustenances by means of a low FODMAP slim down, which removes nourishments like beans and dull vegetables.

Conceding that lectins can be troublesome in high amounts, or when you eat lectin-rich sustenances crude. "In any case, I don't know who eats chickpeas or quinoa crude," she says. Actually, just splashing beans and grains medium-term and cooking them diminishes the measure of lectins that can cause GI trouble. Peeling and de-seeding nightshades can help as well.

In addition, there are a wide range of kinds of lectins. Some are against microbial and may have hostile to disease potential (woot!), while different lectins aren't so bravo. Be that as it may, look into is somewhat touchy on the two sides. "The greater part of research [on lectins] have been creature and in vitro contemplates, not ponders in people,". So take the discoveries with a grain of salt.

# Fact About 6 Foods That Are High In Lectins

1. 1.Red Kidney Beans
2. Wheat
3. 3.Soybeans
4. Peanuts
5. Tomatoes
6. Potatoes.

## Red Kidney Beans

Red kidney beans are among the most extravagant wellsprings of plant-based protein.

They are likewise an awesome wellspring of carbs that are low on the glycemic record (GI).

This implies they discharge their sugars all the more gradually into the blood, causing a slow ascent in glucose as opposed to a sharp spike.

They are likewise high in safe starch and insoluble fiber, which can help with weight reduction and enhance general gut wellbeing.

Red kidney beans contain numerous imperative vitamins and minerals, for example, press, potassium, folate and vitamin K1.

In any case, crude kidney beans additionally contain elevated amounts of a lectin called phytohaemagglutinin.

On the off chance that you eat them crude or undercooked, they can cause extraordinary queasiness, retching and loose bowels. As few as five beans can cause a reaction.

A hemagglutinating unit (hau) is a measure of lectin content. In their crude frame, red kidney beans contain 20,000– 70,000 hau. Once they're altogether cooked, they contain just 200– 400 hau, which is viewed as a protected level.

For whatever length of time that they are appropriately cooked, red kidney beans are a significant and nutritious sustenance that shouldn't be evaded

**Wheat**

Wheat is the staple sustenance for 35% of the total populace.

Refined wheat items have a high glycemic file (GI), which can cause your glucose to spike. They've additionally been stripped of for all intents and purposes all supplements.

Entire wheat has a comparable GI, yet it's higher in fiber, which can effectsly affect gut wellbeing.

A few people experience issues processing gluten, a protein found in wheat. Be that as it may, on the off chance that you endure it, at that point entire wheat can be a decent wellspring of numerous vitamins and minerals, for example, selenium, copper and folate.

Entire wheat likewise contains cell reinforcements, for example, ferulic corrosive, which has been connected to a diminishment in coronary illness.

Crude wheat, particularly wheat germ, is high in lectins, with around 300 mcg of wheat lectins per gram. Notwithstanding, it gives the idea that the lectins are totally wiped out by cooking and handling.

Entire wheat flour has a much lower lectin substance of around 30 mcg for every gram.

When you cook entire wheat pasta, it appears to totally inactivate the lectins, even at temperatures as low as 149°F (65°C). In cooked pasta, lectins are imperceptible.

In addition, examine demonstrates that locally acquired entire wheat pasta doesn't contain any lectins whatsoever, since it's generally presented to warm medications amid generation.

Since most entire wheat items you eat are cooked, it isn't likely that lectins represent a huge issue.

# Soybeans

Soybeans are an awesome wellspring of protein. They are one of the most astounding quality plant-based proteins,
which makes them especially imperative for veggie lovers.
They are a decent wellspring of vitamins and minerals, especially molybdenum, phosphorus and thiamine.
They likewise contain plant mixes called isoflavones, which have been connected to tumor counteractive action and a diminished danger of osteoporosis.
Research demonstrates soybeans can likewise help bring down cholesterol and diminish the danger of creating weight and sort 2 diabetes.
Be that as it may, soybeans are another sustenance that contains elevated amounts of lectins.
Similarly as with red kidney beans, cooking soybeans totally disposes of the lectins. However ensure you cook them for a considerable length of time at a sufficiently high temperature.
Research demonstrates that soybean lectins are totally deactivated when they're bubbled at 212°F (100°C) for no less than 10 minutes.
Conversely, dry or wet warming of soybeans at 158°F (70°C) for a few hours had almost no impact on their lectin content.
Then again, aging and growing are both demonstrated techniques for decreasing lectins.
One examination found that maturing soybeans decreased the lectin content by 95%. Another investigation found that growing diminished the lectin content by 59%.
Matured soybean items incorporate soy sauce, miso and tempeh. Soybean grows are likewise broadly accessible, and can be added to plates of mixed greens or utilized as a part of mix fries.

# Peanuts

Peanuts are really delegated vegetables, and are identified with beans and lentils.

They are high in mono-and polyunsaturated fats, making them an awesome wellspring of vitality.

They are likewise high in protein and an extensive variety of vitamins and minerals, for example, biotin, vitamin E and thiamine.

Peanuts are likewise wealthy in cancer prevention agents, and have been connected to medical advantages like a lessened danger of coronary illness and gallstones.

Not at all like with a portion of alternate nourishments on this rundown, the lectins in peanuts don't give off an impression of being lessened by warming.

An investigation found that after members ate 7 ounces (200 grams) of either crude or simmered peanuts, lectins were found in their blood, showing that they had crossed through from the gut.

One test-tube contemplate found that shelled nut lectins expanded development in tumor cells.

This, nearby the proof that nut lectins can enter the circulation system, has driven a few people to trust that lectins could urge disease to spread in the body.

Be that as it may, this investigation was completed utilizing high dosages of unadulterated lectins put straightforwardly onto tumor cells. There are no examinations up 'til now on the correct impacts in people.

Up until this point, the proof for peanuts' medical advantages and part in disease anticipation is far more grounded than the confirmation for any potential damage they may cause.

# Tomatoes

Tomatoes are a piece of the nightshade family, alongside potatoes, eggplants and ringer peppers.

Tomatoes are high in fiber and wealthy in vitamin C, with one tomato giving roughly 28% of the prescribed day by day allow.

They are likewise a decent wellspring of potassium, folate and vitamin K1.

A standout amongst the most considered mixes in tomatoes is the cancer prevention agent lycopene. It has been found to diminish irritation and coronary illness, and studies have indicated it might ensure against disease.

Tomatoes additionally contain lectins, however there is at present no immediate confirmation they have any negative impacts in people. The accessible investigations have been on creatures or in test tubes.

In one investigation on rats, tomato lectins were found to tie to the gut divider, however they didn't seem to create any harm.

Another examination found that tomato lectins do figure out how to cross the gut and enter the circulatory system once they've been eaten.

Without a doubt, a few people do seem to respond to tomatoes, yet this will probably be because of something many refer to as dust sustenance sensitivity disorder or oral hypersensitivity disorder.

A few people have connected tomatoes and other nightshade vegetables to aggravation, for example, that found in joint pain. Up until this point, no formal research has bolstered this connection.

Lectins have been connected to rheumatoid joint inflammation, however just for the individuals who convey qualities that put them at a high danger of the illness. The examination found no connection between rheumatoid joint inflammation and nightshade vegetables, particularly.

# Potatoes

Potatoes are another individual from the nightshade family. They are an exceptionally prevalent sustenance and are eaten in numerous structures.

Eaten with the skin, potatoes are additionally a decent wellspring of a few vitamins and minerals.

They contain large amounts of potassium, which has been appeared to diminish the danger of coronary illness. They are likewise a rich wellspring of vitamin C and folate.

The skins, specifically, are high in cancer prevention agents, for example, chlorogenic corrosive. This compound has been related with a diminishment in the danger of coronary illness, type 2 diabetes and Alzheimer's malady.

Potatoes have likewise been appeared to build sentiments of totality, which can help with weight reduction. All things considered, it is imperative to consider how they are cooked.

Potatoes are high in lectins that seem, by all accounts, to be impervious to warm. Around 40– half of their lectin content stays in the wake of cooking.

Similarly as with tomatoes, a few people report encountering antagonistic impacts when they eat potatoes. Creature and test-tube considers have demonstrated this could be connected to lectins. In any case, more investigations in people are required.

For the greater part of individuals, potatoes don't cause any antagonistic impacts. Indeed, one examination found that a few assortments of potatoes were connected to a decrease in aggravation.

# Chapter 3: Managing Lectins

The most evident activity is to not eat high sugar nourishments that likewise contain lectins, which you as of now do while on the Bulletproof eating regimen. Likewise, constrain bring down sugar high lectin nightshades, and test your reaction to them with your iPhone utilizing the free Bulletproof Food Sense application.

The following best thing is to mechanically evacuate the parts of the nourishment that have the most lectin in them. This is the reason, all through history, the higher monetary classes would pick white rice over dark colored rice and white flour over entire wheat. Not that you ought to ever eat gluten on the off chance that you are a superior worker, yet in the event that you did, now you know for what reason to

pick the white flour! This is additionally one motivation behind why white rice is positioned higher than dark colored rice on the Bulletproof Diet. Who needs additional fiber when it's enveloped by lectin?

Generally, individuals have utilized an assortment of methods to endeavor to lessen these nourishment poisons. Cooking now and again helps, however a few lectins are made more grounded, for example, red kidney beans, which move toward becoming 5 times more harmful when warmed to 80 degrees Celsius.7 Dry warmth doesn't work extremely well to separate lectins, which is the reason heating with "gluten free" garbanzo bean flour is a terrible thought. The best cooking technique to decimate lectins is weight cooking.

You could likewise have a go at maturing. The main issue is that when you enable microscopic organisms to breakdown proteins, including lectins, you get the production of histamine, which triggers sensitivities. Oh no. In any case, it's smarter to enable microscopic organisms to process the lectin than it is to permit it in your body. This is the reason, on the off chance that you should eat soy, you should stay with matured soy like miso, tempeh, tamari, and natto. In any case, the histamine and phytoestrogens in soy, aged or not, should ward off you in the event that you read this blog! To the extent I can inform, nobody has ever composed regarding how drenching to decrease lectins can build histamine, and uncalled for aging methods can cause the development of form poisons. At that point there's drenching and flushing. Your grandma likely doused beans medium-term, at that point flushed and bubbled them once more, potentially with preparing pop. She may have done this so you, her dazzling grand kid, would have less intestinal gas, yet the purpose behind this impact was that she was expelling a few lectins.

## All That You Need To Know

Not very many sustenances are great.
The vast majority of them have both "great" and "awful" perspectives.
Lectins are among the "awful" things that are every now and again specified.
Lectins are a group of proteins found in basically all sustenances, particularly vegetables and grains.
Visit utilization of a lot of lectins has been appeared to harm the covering of the stomach related framework.
A few people guarantee that this causes expanded gut penetrability and drives immune system infection.
The reality of the matter is that lectins can cause hurt, yet there is a whole other world to the story than we've been told. For instance, it is anything but difficult to dispose of them with the correct arrangement techniques.

## Where Do They Come From?

Lectins are assorted group of starch restricting proteins found in nature. All plants and creatures contain them.
These proteins assume different parts in ordinary physiological capacities, including those of our own bodies.
For instance, they encourage cells and atoms adhere to each other, and perform different capacities identified with the resistant framework.
Albeit all sustenances contain a few lectins, just around 30% of the nourishments we eat contain them in noteworthy sums.
Vegetables (counting beans, soybeans and peanuts) and grains contain the most lectins, trailed by dairy, fish and plants in the nightshade family.
Their capacity in plants isn't clear, however they may have developed as a survival component.

Most plants would prefer not to be eaten, so having these harming particles may debilitate creatures from eating them in huge sums.

Much the same as different creatures, people are powerless against the lethality of lectins. Concentrated sums can cause stomach related problems and long haul medical issues.

On account of the toxin ricin (a lectin from the castor oil plant), they can even reason passing.

## Eating Routine Without The Die

1. Health risks of being overweight
2. Psychological Consequences Of Being Overweight
3. Loss of Energy and Joy for Life

## I.Health Risks Of Being Overweight

Individuals who effectively get more fit frequently inspire themselves to do so by keeping the health benefits of weight loss solidly in mind. Overweight and obese people are at increased danger of developing genuine and sometimes life-threatening diseases as they age, including:

- Heart Disease
- Heart Attack
- Heart Failure
- Coronary Artery Disease (CAD)
- High Blood Pressure
- Angina
- Abnormal heartbeat
- Cholesterol problems (leading to heart sickness)
- Elevated LDL ("terrible") cholesterol and triglycerides levels
- Lowered beneficial HDL ("good") cholesterol levels,

- Stroke
- Type 2 Diabetes (the kind you develop rather than are born with)
- Cancers (prostate, gallbladder, colorectal, breast, endometrial and kidney)
- Liver issues (such as an enlarged liver, cirrhosis or a fatty liver)
- Gastroesophageal ("Acid") Reflux Disease (GERD)
- Sleep Apnea (Snoring and trouble breathing while dozing)
- Asthma Shallow breathing (Pickwickian syndrome which can lead to heart disease)
- Arthritis

## Gallstones (In Ladies)

Reproductive problems (sporadic periods, increased birth defects, particularly neural tube defects, and an expanded risk of death of the mother and child).

## Memory And Learning Problems (In Men)

The risk of developing some of these serious sicknesses (type 2 diabetes, arthritis) tends to increase as a person gets heavier. How fat is distributed on the body has important implications for health risks as well. Fat that collects around the abdomen and stomach areas (e.g., the so called "beer belly" or "love handle") predicts more genuine health issues than fats that accumulates around the hips and thighs. Men with midsection estimations of more than 40 inches or lady with waist measurements greater than 35 inches are at higher risk for developing type 2 diabetes, high blood weight, high cholesterol, and coronary conduit sickness than are normal weight individuals or those whose fat accumulates around the hips.

## Ii.Psychological Consequences Of Being Overweight

Psychological consequences of being overweight or obese can include lowered self-esteem and anxiety, and more serious disorders such as depression and eating disorders such as binge eating, bulimia and anorexia. The reasons for why this is so aren't hard to fathom. Modern culture is singular in the way that it worships youthful slim, toned bodies. With rare exceptions, only thin, proportional bodies are considered sexy. Obese or overweight people are looked down upon. It's easy to feel bad about one's self, to become depressed or anxious or to to develop obsessions around eating control when one's culture makes it clear that the way one appears is wholly undesirable.

One doesn't have to be overweight to get into psychological trouble with eating, either. Eating is pleasurable, and because this is true, all manner of people (fat and thin both) end up using eating as a ready source of emotional comfort when they are feeling stressed out. It comes as no surprise that such stress-induced eating leads to weight gain, which in turn leads many people (especially women) to feel still worse about themselves, motivating still more stress-based eating and additional weight gain. All too often, stress-based comfort eating becomes a vicious cycle and downward spiral.

## Iii.Loss Of Energy And Joy For Life

If the negative health and shame aspects of being overweight aren't enough, overweight people also tend to have less energy than their normal weight peers. Because it takes them more effort than their peers to be active, they tend to gravitate towards low-activity lifestyles and become sedentary. An unfortunate circle develops wherein the less active people become the greater their risk of gaining still more weight, and the more weight people gain, the less likely they are to become more active. Life stresses seem more overwhelming as exercise (which could begin the process of reversing this downward spiral of decreasing energy levels) is avoided and a major opportunity for the reduction of muscle tension, stress and anxiety is lost. Over time, even ordinary tasks of daily life like going up a flight of stairs can lead to exhaustion and a sense of premature aging.

However am going to share some testimonies of people who have gone through the weight loss diet:

HERE IS:

# Sam From Oakland, Dc

Hi, I have lost 90 lbs. during the last year using weight watchers and walking 4 to 5 times per week. I lost an average of 8 lbs per month over 12 months and am keeping it off. I am 5'6" and now weigh 135 lbs., which is a normal weight according to the AMA, the websites from health insurance carriers, etc. So far, I have continued to exercise and "count points" according to the weight watcher maintenance program and I have kept my weight under 140 lbs. I realize that I look very different and people notice and frequently comment about the weight loss. Certainly I enjoy it when someone says, "Gee, you look great!" However, there is also a tendency for some people to assume that it is OK to make rather personal comments about my body size and weight (previous and current), even in front of other people. I find this overly personal, particularly at work. I am beginning to feel anxious and uptight when people make any comments about my weight loss because I never know how intrusive or embarrassing the comments are going to become. In particular, it is very uncomfortable to hear people say "Oh my God, you've lost SO much weight!" or "You aren't trying to lose any more, are you?" or "Are you STILL losing weight?" or "How much weight have you lost?" - "you look SO different". It sometimes feels that I have very little privacy about my body, even at work, which is a professional setting. The comments are beginning to feel hostile, rather than supportive. I have begun to ask some of my co-workers not to comment. Generally, once I say something, a light seems to go off and people usually understand that discussing another person's body might be inappropriate. I have been looking on-line for comments or research about this to see if other people who have lost weight have this problem. I don't want to whine about achieving an important goal, but it does seems like our culture is so obsessed about weight and being fat, that people just can't believe it when someone actually does lose all the weight. I am not anorexic, nor do I believe that I have any eating disorder or that there is anything wrong with me. I have done a lot of research about what is a healthy weight and I believe that I am now a normal weight. My husband is very supportive and believes that I am healthy. I feel healthy. However, some of the people who have known me for a long time seem to be having difficulty getting used to the way I look now.

# Lizzy From Los Angeles

Hi, my name is LIZZY and I am a Los Angeles native but live in Mississippi now. I have been having the same problem as you regarding my weight loss. In March of 2006, I was 183 lbs, now as of August 2007, I am at my goal weight of 115 lbs and plan to keep it off for life. I am really happy about my accomplishment. Others have been excited about my weight loss as well - FOR A WHILE, ANYWAY. When I first started losing, people would give me compliments, which I loved, but then when I started to get closer to my goal, people I know everywhere, particularly at work, started telling me that I didn't need to lose any more weight, but I wasn't satisfied with where I was. I still get good compliments even now on how good I look, but I wanted to get to "MY" goal weight, not the weight where they wanted me to be. I started getting comments like the ones you were receiving," You're not still on a diet, are you?", and "You don't need to lose any more weight." So I definitely know where you are coming from. It really does feel uncomfortable at times. It even got to a point where I would feel uncomfortable to eat in front of others because I felt as though they were watching my every move and everything I was eating. When I would bring my lunch to work, everyone would ask me all the time, "Crystal, what did you bring for lunch today?", which was okay at first, but eventually it got to be very, very annoying. I am so glad that I didn't let anyone stop me from achieving my goal of 115 lbs. If I would have listened to everyone, I would not be where I am today. Don't get me wrong, I'm not saying that a person shouldn't listen to advice because people do mean well most of the time when they give you advice, but sometime listening to others will hinder your success. So my advice to you and all others who are winning the battle of weight, "Go for it!" "Whatever weight goal you have set for yourself, doesn't give up until you have reached it." Don't let others discourage or persuade you otherwise.

# Chapter 4: Why Do We Gain Weight?

The 'calorie' is a unit of measurement of the energy contained within foods. Living bodies require a certain number of calories each day as fuel. Food calories are metabolized (burned up) by the body to create energy necessary to keep it going. Calories in excess of what the body needs as fuel get stored in the form of fat reserves which buffer the body against the possibility that calories might be hard to get a hold of in the future. Stored fat calories get burned and used up when no food is available and the body must look for alternative sources of fuel.

People gain weight and get fat when they consistently eat more calories than their bodies require meeting daily demands. That excess calories get stored as fat is an adaptive evolutionary response inherited from times not that long ago when food was less abundantly available and people had to work far harder to get a hold of what food was available. People who were able to store food in the form of fat when food was readily available were more likely to survive and reproduce through times when food was difficult to get than were their skinny peers. Because of this evolutionary advantage, our bodies have developed so that it is rewarding and natural for us to eat a lot of food when it is available. Despite being efficient stores of body fat, ancestral humans were not often obese as they had to work hard to eat and in the process burned up what calories they ate. However, the dramatic agricultural and technological changes of the past two thousand years have made food extremely easy to obtain and evolution has not been able to keep pace in so short a time span. At this juncture we are required to use our intellect to understand our bodies' instincts and to develop a more twenty-first century appropriate relationship with food.

One of the biggest healthy-living #likeaboss buzzkills out there is when you've realized you've put on extra weight and have no idea why. If your skinny jeans fit just a couple of months ago, and you haven't done anything differently, what gives?

You eat healthy foods, stay loyal to your boot camp class and drink plenty of water, but the pounds have crept onto your frame. And for no good reason! Or is there?

While your exercise and eat-right efforts are still super important for you to achieve flat belly success, there are a number of things that can cause your waistline to expand many of which are downright sneaky or out of your control. (Cue the groans.) But don't panic! To help you kick pesky poundage to the curb, we uncovered some of the top flat belly saboteurs and asked experts how to overcome each ...so you can get back to your slimmer self. And after you see how simple it can be to get on a path toward your ideal weight, be sure to check out this Weight Loss Tricks You Haven't Tried!

## 1. Your Thyroid Is Sluggish

The thyroid, a gland in the neck that sits above the Adam's apple, regulates a wide range of bodily functions including metabolism. But sometimes, for a variety of reasons, your thyroid may become under-active and result in a condition called hypothyroidism. One of the many symptoms of the condition? You guessed it, weight gain. The worst part is that the condition often develops slowly, so many people don't notice the symptoms of the disease until they're full blown, says The National Institute of Diabetes and Digestive and Kidney Diseases. It gets worse: If a thyroid issue is to blame for your weight gain, it doesn't matter how diligently you're dieting and working out; it will be near impossible to shed the pounds.

Do This: Take a trip to the MD. "If you've suddenly put on weight for no apparent reason, I suggest you see a doctor so a medical professional can decide whether it is a thyroid issue or another cause," says 'Biggest Loser' dietitian Cheryl Forberg.

## 2. You Overeat Healthy Foods

When losing your love handles is the goal, portion size is just as important as eating healthy. The reason: Many nutritious foods like avocados, oatmeal, quinoa, dark chocolate, nuts and nut butters can lead to weight gain when eaten in excess.

Do This: Unless it's a fruit or a vegetable, don't make the assumption that the healthy food you're eating is low calorie. Next time you're whipping up a meal, remember these three portion control cues: 1.) A helping of nut butter or shredded cheese should be no larger than a ping-pong ball; 2.) a true serving of rice and pasta is about the size of your fist; and 3.) lean meats should be about the size of a deck of cards. Sticking to the recommended serving size can help zap away excess pounds.

## 3. You're Dehydrated

Earlier this year, a University of Utah study found that drinking two cups of water before each meal could significantly accelerate weight loss. So it should come as no surprise that not drinking enough H20 can have the opposite effect on your waistline. "Not only does water give us energy and help maintain body temperature, but it also helps us feel fuller," says Forberg. "Not drinking enough water can cause us to eat excess calories that could lead to weight gain. Plus, when you're dehydrated, the body will conserve water for vital body functions, which can result in water retention and a higher number on the scale."

Do This: Keep hydration and pounds at bay by sipping continuously throughout the day. And when your taste buds finally tire of plain H2O, whip up one of these 50 Best Detox Waters for Fat Burning and Weight Loss.

## 4. You're Depressed

and you're taking medication to treat it. "As many as 25 percent of people taking certain antidepressants report gaining ten pounds or more," says Alissa Rumsey, Registered Dietitian and Spokesperson for the Academy of Nutrition and Dietetics. "Some medications may cause food cravings, especially for carbohydrates, and some find that their medication increases their appetite. The drugs may affect metabolism negatively as well." And since depression is often accompanied by a disinterest in food, another pool of thought is that once antidepressants become effective, people regain their appetites and overeat.
Do This: "Switching medications can often help since certain types are more apt to cause weight gain than others. However, if you change medications, it may not aid your depression as effectively. It can be a lot of trial and error," adds Rumsey.

## 5. You Avoid The Scale

Of all the little white lies, the expression "what you don't know can't hurt you" is one of the worst, regarding weight loss. However, when we're talking about weight gain, ignorance could be the very reason behind your ever-tightening waistband. "When you avoid the scale because you don't want to know the number, that's when you get into trouble. This is especially true in the winter months, when we're more apt to indulge in comfort food and cover ourselves with bulky sweaters," says registered dietitian Christine M. Palumbo.

Do This: If you want to shed the extra poundage, you've got to lay off the treats, increase your activity throughout the day and hop on a scale at least once a week if not two or three, to monitor your progress. "I recommend weighing in on Monday, Wednesday, and Friday," says Palumbo. "If Monday is a bit higher than usual, all the better for getting back on track for the upcoming week. And Friday is good because if you're a bit on the high side then, well, it's all the more incentive to stay-the-course for the weekend and not goes too crazy."

## 6. You're Obsessed With Spinning

There's no denying that working out is an important weight loss factor, but oddly enough, thinking about your upcoming sweat sessions too often can make it more difficult to lose weight. Research indicates that when your favorite spin class is always on the brain, you apt to consume more calories likely because you assume you'll just blast it away during the hill and sprint sections of your class. And sadly, for the average gym rat or spin-devotee, this is hardly ever the case.

Do This: Set it and forget it! At the beginning of each month, sit down with your iCal and plan out your workouts for the next month. This way you aren't constantly thinking about your post-work gym sessions; you can just reference your calendar and go. To fuel your weight loss further, avoid excessive noshing and pick up some of these pre-workout snacks tailored to your fitness routine.

## 7. You Don't Check Yourself Out

Is your obsession with Reese's and Pringles derailing your weight loss efforts? It might be if you're not using the self-checkout kiosks at the grocery store. Let us explain: According to a study by IHL Consulting Group, impulse purchases dipped 32.1 percent for women and 16.7 percent for men when they were the ones to scan their items and swipe their credit card. Although not all impulse buys are bad for your belly, a whopping 80 percent of candy and 61 percent of salty-snack purchases are unplanned.

Do This: Next time you're at the grocery store, head to the self-checkout line. Switching up your routine may just be your ticket to slim-down success.

## 8. You Stay Up Late

You eat right and exercise but, sadly, nearly all of your efforts are negated if you're staying up all night catching up on 'Empire.' In study after study, shorter amounts of sleep are associated with higher BMI levels and larger waistlines. The primary reason? "Lack of sleep can lead to increased levels of the hunger hormone ghrelin, and decreased levels of leptin, the satiety hormone," explains Rumsey. "Research also shows that when we're sleep-deprived, our brains respond more strongly to junk food and have less of an ability to practice portion control."

Do This: Rumsey assures us that after a week or two of adequate sleep which she defines as seven to eight hours per evening the surge of hunger and cravings should subside. And to boost your calorie burn before hitting the sheets.

## 9. Your Job Is Really Stressful

We don't mean suggest that you pass the buck, but your demanding boss may be to blame for your expanding waistline. "The hormone cortisol is released when our body is under stress that causes triglycerides to be relocated to visceral fat cells, increasing storage of belly fat," explains Rumsey. "Elevated cortisol levels also cause an increase in blood glucose, while suppressing the effects of insulin, leading to constant feelings of hunger and can lead to overeating. To make matters worse, all of that unused blood glucose is eventually stored as body fat."

Do This: Discuss your workload with your manager. Alternatively, come into the office early when no one is around to bug you. This will allow you to get a head start on the day's assignments without your Chatty Cathy cubical neighbor annoying you. To relax even more, take a mid-day break.

## 10. You Don't Eat Enough Protein

Consuming enough protein is important for two reasons: Since it digests more slowly than refined carbohydrates, it's satiating and staves off overeating. It also helps maintain lean muscle mass. "If you aren't consuming enough protein to keep your muscles and cells healthy, the body ends up breaking down muscle to access the nutrients it needs and this spells trouble. Less muscle mass means a slower metabolism, which over time can cause weight gain," explains Rumsey.

Do This: To keep your metabolism going strong, stock your kitchen with enough protein in your store.

## 11. You Never Indulge

If every time you have a cookie craving you buy a low-fat package, you may be doing your body a disservice sounds counterintuitive, we know. When food manufacturers trim the fat, they often pump their snacks full of sugar and additives that can leave you feeling unsatisfied and craving more not what you want if you're trying to reverse recent weight gain.

Do This: To get back to a trimmer version of you, eat the real thing, but downsize your portion. If you love ice cream, for example, skip the fro-yo and have a small scoop of premium.

## 12. You're Taking Medication

From beta-blockers to birth control pills, and everything in between, there's a long, long list of medications that can cause your waistline to bulge. And if you think your Rx is to blame for your ever-expanding waistline, you're not alone. "Weight issues are often a primary reason for non-compliance with treatment," Palumbo tells us. "Some drugs stimulate the appetite or slow the body's metabolism. Others cause fluid retention or enough drowsiness to reduce physical activity, which can trigger weight gain."

Do This: This is important, so listen up: "If you suspect your drug is causing weight gain, never stop taking it. Instead, make an appointment with your healthcare provider and ask if there might be an equally effective alternative that doesn't affect your weight. Everyone reacts to medications differently, so trying something else may help.

# Chapter 5: Nutrition And Weight Loss

Most weight loss programs begin with a reducing diet (designed to promote weight loss) which creates its effect by limiting how much of different types of foods one can eat. There is a bewildering number of reducing diet styles, however. Some recommend a simple reduction in the total amount of food consumed, while others recommend specific reductions of particular types of foods consumed (breads and pastas, for instance). Knowledge of basic nutrition concepts helps us to understand why the varieties of recommendations exist.

### THE FOOD PYRAMID

A good starting place for diet and nutrition information is the USDA's research-based Food Pyramid guide for selecting a healthy diet.

**The food pyramid starts by dividing foods into the following six food groups:**

- Grains
- Vegetables
- Fruits
- Oils
- Milk
- Meat & Beans

The six groups are then arranged into a pyramid shape to indicate the relative proportions of each food that people should eat each day. For example, the Grains (bread, cereals, rice and pasta) group takes up a larger percentage of the pyramid's area than other groups to indicate that proportionally more servings of bread, cereals, rice and pasta are appropriate to eat each day versus other groups. Importantly, not just any grain is recommended. At least half of the grains eaten in a given day should be 'whole' grains, which contain the grain germ (fertile seed part), and the bran (hard outer seed coating). Look for whole wheat breads and pastas when making food choices, if possible.

The Fruits and Vegetables group's area is smaller than the Grains group, but larger than the Milk and Meat & Beans groups, suggesting that more fruits and vegetables are to be consumed than milk, meat or beans for balanced nutrition. The types of fruit and vegetable choices made are important as well. Whole, fresh fruit is much better for you than fruit juice. Dark green and orange vegetables such as spinach and carrots are in general better for you than vegetables that do not have these colors, and fresh vegetables are in general better for you than canned vegetables. When choosing dairy or meats to eat, the pyramid suggests that you choose lower fat varieties. When choosing oils and fats to use for cooking and eating, the pyramid indicates that liquid choices (such as olive oil) are better than solid choices (such as butter, margarine, or shortening). The Oils group is the smallest of all the groups, indicating that as a percentage of your total diet, relatively few oils should be consumed.

For the first time ever, the pyramid now includes a physical exercise component as part of the essential food groups, to indicate that regular physical exercise for at least 30 minutes a day, most days of the week (60 minutes a day for children and teens!), is vital for everyone's health.

**Carbs, Fats and Protein**

The six food groups recognized in the food pyramid may be each very different in origin, composition and taste, but they all contain nutrients necessary for building and maintaining bodily health. There are six classes of necessary nutrients found in foods: carbohydrates, fats, protein, vitamins, minerals and water. Working together, these nutrients perform three vital life functions: they provide energy, they promote body growth and maintenance, and they assist in regulating bodily processes.

Carbohydrates, fats and proteins work together to provide us with energy. Proteins, fats, vitamins, minerals and water promote growth and maintenance and are necessary for appropriate body process regulation. All six nutrient classes must be present in sufficient amounts at all times or the body will not function properly.

Different nutrient classes contain different amounts of calories. For instance, carbohydrates and proteins provide only 4 calories per gram while fat provides 9 calories per gram. This is why high fat foods are more 'fattening' than lower fat foods; they are more calorically dense.

With the exception of water, each nutrient class contains a variety of different subtypes of that nutrient. Some of these nutrient subtypes can be better for health than others. For example, within the fats class, there are saturated fats, mono-unsaturated fats and poly-unsaturated fats. Eating a diet high in saturated fats (such as are found in butter, lard, and shortening) is known to increase LDL (bad) cholesterol levels and increase the risk for cardiovascular disease. Trans-fatty acids (man-made saturated fats produced via a process called hydrogenation), found in most margarines and store-bought baked goods, are now thought to pose similar health risks. On the other hand, mono-unsaturated and poly-unsaturated fats (such as occur in olive oil) help to lower LDL cholesterol.

Like fats, carbohydrate subtypes are not all equally nutritious. Foods rich in refined sugar and flour (white bread, cakes, cookies, etc.) provide 'empty' calories as they are mostly devoid of nutritional value. In contrast, complex unrefined carbohydrates such as those found in whole grain products (brown rice, bran, whole wheat bread, etc.) and fruits and vegetables provide essential nutrients as well as fiber in addition to providing energy. Fiber comes in two helpful varieties. Insoluble fibers helps to keep the digestive and eliminatory tract functioning regularly, while soluble fiber helps to keep the arteries clean by reducing LDL cholesterol in the bloodstream.

All nutrients, including carbohydrates, fats and proteins, are essential for life and should be present in a healthy diet. Since all classes of nutrients are necessary the wisdom of severely limiting or eliminating any category is questionable. Rather than attempting to eliminate nutrient classes as some reducing diets seem to suggest, the wisest course is to select a diet based heavily on the healthier types of nutrients from each nutrient class. Such a diet includes fresh fruits and vegetables, whole grain breads and cereals, lean meats, fish and poultry, low fat or nonfat dairy products, and the sparing use of healthy fats such as olive oil. Refined sugars, white flour, and partially-hydrogenated oils should be avoided. Less nutritious (but still delicious) foods, including steaks, hot dogs and sausages, cream and butter, and cake and ice cream can be eaten on an occasional basis but should not become staples of an everyday diet.

## Habits That Can Help You Lose Weight

Weight control is all about making small changes that you can live with forever. As you incorporate these minor adjustments into your lifestyle, you'll begin to see how they can add up to big calorie savings and weight loss. Here are my top 10 habits to help you turn your dream of weight loss into a reality:
1. Evaluate your eating habits. Are you eating late at night, nibbling while cooking, finishing the kids' meals? Take a look around, and it will be easy to identify a few behaviors you can change that will add up to big calorie savings.
2. If you fail to plan, plan to fail. You need a strategy for your meals and snacks. Pack healthful snacks for the times of day that you know you are typically hungry and can easily stray from your eating plan.
3. Always shop with a full belly. It's a recipe for disaster to go into the grocery store when you are hungry. Shop from a

prepared list so impulse buying is kept to a minimum. Eating right starts with stocking healthy food in your pantry and refrigerator.

4. Eat regular meals. Figure out the frequency of your meals that works best in your life and stick to it. Regular meals help prevent bingeing.

5. Eat your food sitting down at a table, and from a plate. Food eaten out of packages and while standing is forgettable. You can wind up eating lots more than if you sit down and consciously enjoy your meals.

6. Serve food onto individual plates, and leave the extras back at the stove. Bowls of food on the table beg to be eaten, and it takes incredible will power not to dig in for seconds. Remember, it takes about 20 minutes for your mind to get the signal from your belly that you are full.

7. Eat slowly, chew every bite, and savor the taste of the food. Try resting your fork between bites and drinking plenty of water with your meals.

8. Don't eat after dinner. This is where lots of folks pack on the extra pounds. If you are hungry, try satisfying your urge with a non-caloric beverage or a piece of hard candy. Brushing your teeth after dinner helps reduce the temptation to eat again.

9. If you snack during the day, treat the snack like a mini-meal. The most nutritious snacks contain complex carbohydrates and a small amount of protein and fat.

10. Start your day with breakfast. It is the most important meal of the day. After a long night's rest, your body needs the fuel to get your metabolism going and give you energy for the rest of the day.

# Chapter 6: Lectin-Free Vegan And Non-Vegan Recipes

## 1. Sweet Potato Hash

A breakfast recipe of sweet potatoes with a savoury touch with addition of spices and garlic mixed with scrambled eggs. You can serve it with a side of tempeh bacon!

Prep time: 10 mins
Cook time: 40 mins
Total time: 50 mins

**Yield**: 2-4 servings

Ingredients:

- 2 peeled medium sweet potatoes, cubed in small pieces
- 2 tbsps. avocado oil or olive oil
- 1 tsp. smoked paprika
- ½ tsp. turmeric
- ½ tsp. sea salt
- ½ tsp. onion powder
- ¼- ½ tsp. freshly ground black pepper
- 2 minced garlic cloves
- Sliced Scallions

Directions:

1. Preheat the oven to 400 degrees F.
2. Take a medium or large bowl, toss sweet potatoes with oil. Add sea salt, paprika, turmeric, black pepper and onion powder and mix well to combine. Transfer the sweet

potatoes onto a sheet pan. Divide the sweet potatoes into two pans if the pan becomes over crowded.
3. Bake for about 20 minutes.
4. Take out the pan from the oven and gently stir sweet potatoes so that you don't smash them. Place the pan back into the oven and bake for 10-15 minutes more.
5. Take out the pan again and add minced garlic cloves and bake for 5 more minutes. You can turn off the oven at this point if the color of your sweet potatoes gets too dark. You just have to barely cook the garlic cloves until it smells good.
6. Take it out of the oven and top with scallions. Serve it hot with tofu scramble (vegan option) or scrambled eggs, tempeh bacon and a drizzle of hot sauce if desired.

**Nutrition information per serving:** 176 Calories, 14g carbs, 16g protein and 8g fats.

## 2. Homemade Granola Bars (Grain-Free, Lectin-Free)

Satisfy your hunger with these lectin free granola bars. They are the best option to be eaten during school or office time and keep you full!

Prep time 5 mins
Total time 5 mins
**Yield:** 8+ bars

Ingredients:

- 1 cup pecans
- ½ cup almond butter
- ¼ cup almond or pecan flour
- ¼ cup coconut flour
- ¼ cup coconut flakes
- 8 dates
- 2 tbsps. almond milk
- 1 tbsp. dairy-free chocolate chips
- 1 tbsp. hemp seeds
- 1 tbsp. melted coconut oil
- 1 tsp. vanilla extract
- 1 tsp. cinnamon
- ¼ tsp. salt

Directions:

1. Add the first 6 ingredients in a food processor and process until converted into finely ground meal.
2. Add the remaining ingredients and process again until well-combined.

3. Prepare a bread pan or small rectangular container with parchment. Press the mixture into the container so that it adheres together.
4. Cover it with a cling film or a lid and place it in the refrigerator for at least 30 minutes. Cut it into slices and enjoy!

**Nutrition information per serving:** 471 calories, 64g carbs, 10g protein and 20g fats.

# 3. Lectin-Free Vegan Taco "Meat"

Try this easy lectin-free vegan taco meat recipe that will require only 5 minutes for preparation.

Prep time: 5 mins
Total time: 5 mins

Yield: 1 ½ cups

Ingredients:

- **2 cups** organic walnuts
- 10 teaspoons organic extra-virgin olive oil
- 1/2 teaspoon Himalayan pink salt
- 1 teaspoon organic cumin powder
- 1 teaspoon organic chipotle powder
- 1 teaspoon organic chili powder

Directions:

1. Combine all the ingredients by processing in a food processor until the walnuts break into tiny pieces. Avoid over processing.
2. Add seasonings according to your taste.
3. You can use it as a wrap filling or taco filling or for topping on nachos, avocado, baked sweet potato, salad etc.
4. Store it in an air tight container in the refrigerator.
5. **Enjoy!**

**Nutrition information per serving**: 540 calories, 50g carbs, 65g protein and 36g fats

## 4. Cinnamon Cassava Flour Pancakes

This lectin free recipe yields light and fluffy cinnamon pancakes. These are made with cassava flour and goat's milk kefir.

Prep Time 35 minutes
**Cook Time** 35 minutes
Total Time 35 minutes

**Yield:** 4 servings

Ingredients:
- 1 cup cassava flour
- 2 tbsps. monk's fruit sweetener
- 1 tbsp. baking powder
- 1 tsp. cinnamon plus more for serving
- ¼ tsp. sea salt
- 1/8 tsp. nutmeg
- 1 ¼ cup goat's milk kefir or almond/coconut yogurt at room temperature
- ½ tsp. vanilla extract
- 2 large eggs
- 3 tbsps. melted butter + extra for serving
- ¼ cup water

Directions:
1. Set the non-stick griddle to medium or low heat for preheating purpose.
2. Mix together the sweetener, baking powder, flour, nutmeg, sea salt, cinnamon in a bowl until well-combined. Add in the kefir or yogurt, eggs, vanilla and water in a separate large bowl and mix well. Mix in the butter into the kefir mixture.

3. Mix the wet mixture and dry mixture in a large bowl until well combined.
4. Pour the batter over the hot griddle using a ¼ cup and make 2-3 pancakes at a time. Allow them to cook until bubbles start appearing and color changes from the undersides. Flip them using a spatula and cook for one more minute. Repeat the same procedure using more butter.
5. Serve hot and enjoy. However, you can transfer them to a warm oven by covering them with a damp towel so that they remain warm.

**Nutrition information per serving**: 355 calories, 45g carbs, 19g protein and 25g fats.

## 5. Cilantro Lime Salmon Burgers {Paleo, Gluten-Free & Lectin-Free}

Try this super easy lectin-free recipe at home by just mixing everything together to make patties and let them cool!

Prep time: 1 hour 20 minutes
Cook time: 10 minutes
Total time: 1 hour 30 minutes
Yield: 6-8 burgers

Ingredients:

- 1 pound wild caught salmon, finely ground
- 1 large egg
- 1/3 cup chopped fresh cilantro
- ¼ cup finely chopped onion
- Lemon juice of 1 medium lemon
- 1 tbsp. mayonnaise (made with avocado oil)
- 1 tbsp. organic coconut flour
- 1 minced garlic clove
- ½ tsp. sea salt
- 1/8 tsp. crushed red pepper flakes
- Avocado oil

Directions:

1. Add all the ingredients in a bowl and mix well.
2. Divide the mixture into 6-8 equal portions and shape into patties.
3. Place the patties in the freezer for 1 hour.
4. Allow the patties to grill over medium heat until cooked thoroughly in avocado oil as required.
5. Enjoy fresh by making burgers with addition of some veggies of your choice.

**Nutrition information per serving:** 338 calories, 17g carbs, 48.9g protein and 26.2 g fats.

# 6.Tasty Chewy Gingerbread In A Mug

Fill your gut with this lectin free, tasty and chewy Ginger bread in a mug! Do make some extra to share it as gift to your neighbours!

Prep Time: 5 minutes
Cook Time: 1 minute
Total Time: 6 minutes

Yield: 1 **serving**

Ingredients:

- 1 tbsp. softened butter
- 1 tbsp. coconut flour
- 1 tbsp. cassava flour or tigernut
- ½ tsp. baking powder
- ½ tsp. ground ginger
- ¼ tsp. cinnamon powder
- 1 pinch of each cloves, allspice, and nutmeg
- 2 tsp. maple-flavored erythritol syrup
- ½ tsp. apple cider vinegar
- ½ tbsp. water
- 1 lightly beaten egg (large)

Directions:

1. Add butter, coconut flour, baking powder, cassava flour/tigernut, cinnamon powder, ginger and spices in a microwave safe mug and beat all the ingredients well.
2. Pour in the syrup, water, egg, cider vinegar and mix it well using a fork until the batter turns smooth.
3. Place it in the microwave and set time up to 1.5 minutes and allow it to microwave. Using a knife scrape around the edges

of the mug and then dish out the muffin onto a plate. Divide it in half. Pour over some butter and sprinkle cinnamon powder.

**Nutrition information per serving:** 236.4 calories, 12.5 carbs, 21.44g proteins and 15g fats.

# 7. Lectin-Free Vegan Shirataki Angel Hair Pasta With Creamy Chipotle Avocado Sauce

Prep time: 5 mins
Total time: 5 mins
**Yield:** 2 servings

Ingredients:

- 2 packs of Shirataki Angel Hair Pasta

**For the sauce:**

- 2 organic avocados
- ¼ cup organic extra-virgin olive oil
- 2 tbsp. organic lemon juice
- ½ - 1 tsp. organic ground chipotle powder
- ¼ - ½ tsp. Himalayan pink salt

**Directions:**

**For pasta:**

1. Cook pasta as per directions given on the package.

**For the preparation of sauce:**

1. Add all the ingredients in a blender and process until it smoothens and turns creamy.
2. Add seasonings according to your taste.

Assembly:

1. Take a medium sized bowl and add in the prepared pasta.
2. Pour in the sauce and gently toss it with the noodles for even distribution.
3. Give it a finishing touch with chopped fresh cilantro.
4. Serve it warm and enjoy!

**Nutrition information per serving:** 357 calories, 48g carb, 22g proteins and 30g fats.

# 8. Lectin-Free Cesar Salad

A classy lectin-free Caesar salad with a crisp of romaine lettuce tossed in rich salad dressing of lemon olive oil. You can serve it with Italian herb crusted tempeh.

Total time: 30 minutes
Yield: 2 servings

Ingredients

**For Caesar Salad**

- 1 large head romaine lettuce
- 2 small minced garlic cloves
- 5-6 tbsps. of extra virgin olive oil
- 2 tbsps. of lemon juice
- 2 tbsps. of nutritional yeast
- 1 tsp. Dijon mustard
- 6 drops of liquid stevia
- Salt to taste

**For Italian Crusted Tempeh**

- 6 oz. tempeh
- 2 tbsps. of olive oil
- 2 tsps. of nutritional yeast
- ¼ tsp. of truffle salt
- ¼ tsp. Italian seasoning
- 1/8 tsp. freshly ground black pepper

Directions:
1. Combine garlic, 5 tbsp. olive oil, yeast, lemon, stevia, mustard and salt in a food processor and blend well until it

gets smooth. Add another tablespoon of olive oil if dressing is still thick.
2. Enclose the dressing in an airtight container and allow it to cool in refrigerator for at least 30 minutes or 1 hour.
3. Cut the romaine lettuce to the required bite sized pieces.
4. Wash the cut lettuce in a large raised colander. Transfer the colander into a large bowl and transfer the whole contraption in refrigerator while preparing tempeh.
5. Combine truffle, yeast, salt and pepper and Italian seasonings in a small bowl. Place it aside.
6. Take a medium pan and add tempeh and water that fills up to ¾ of the way up the tempeh. Place it over high heat and bring it to boil until all the water evaporates. Reduce the heat to medium and transfer the tempeh to a cutting board.
7. Sprinkle the spice mixture on all the sides of the tempeh making sure that the mixture sticks well to the tempeh.
8. Take a pan and pour in 2 tbsps. of olive oil. Allow it to simmer. Add tempeh and cook for 2-3 minutes per side until the color changes to golden brown. Turn off the flame and cut the tempeh into strips onto a cutting board. Place the strips aside.
9. Toss the lettuce and dressing together in a bowl for at least a minute for even distribution of salad dressing.
10. Equally divide the dressed lettuce onto two platters and serve with tempeh strips. Eat fresh and enjoy!

**7.Nutrition information per serving:** 360 calories, 48 g carbs, 35g protein and 32g fats.

# 9. Lectin Free Pasta Recipe

This easy lectin free pasta recipe tastes just like fresh egg noodles. Do give it a try!

Prep Time: 10 minutes
**Cook Time :** 10 minutes
Total Time: 20 minutes

**Yield:** 2 servings

Ingredients:

- 1 cup tapioca flour + extra for dusting
- 1 cup almond flour
- 1 tsp. kosher salt
- 2 large eggs
- Olive oil as required

Directions:

1. Combine almond flour, tapioca and salt in a bowl.
2. Crack in the eggs by making a well within the flour mixture. Beat the eggs well using a fork and incorporate more and more flour.
3. After incorporating egg, knead using your hands by adding some more tapioca flour if the dough is still sticky. Divide the dough into 3 parts.
4. Dust the rolling pin and the cutting board with the tapioca flour. Take the first part of the dough and dust it with some tapioca flour and roll it out into 1/8-inch thickness. Cut the dough carefully into desired thickness of noodles using a pizza cutter.

5. Boil 4 quarts of water with a drizzle of olive oil in a large pot. Once it begins to boil, add in the noodles and cook for about 2 minutes
6. Remove the noodles from the pot using a slotted spoon and strain it by placing in pasta strainer. Pour over some olive oil to prevent the noodles from sticking. Repeat the process with the remining dough.

**Nutrition information per serving:** 142 calories, 32g carbs, 5g proteins and 20g fats.

## 10. Grilled Sirloin Steak And Leeks With Arugula-Oregano Dressing

Before putting your grill away for the summer, you must try this lectin free recipe of grilled Sirloin steak by incorporating some green veggies.

Prep time: 20 minutes
Total time: 20 minutes

**Yield:** 4 servings

Ingredients:

- 1-pound sirloin steak divided into 2 pieces
- ¾ tsp. freshly ground black pepper
- 6 tbsps. of olive oil, divided
- 1 bunch of trimmed leeks
- 5 cups of baby greens
- 2 cups of loosely packed baby arugula
- 2 tsps. dried oregano
- 1 chopped garlic clove
- 2 tbsps. of red wine vinegar
- 2 tbsps. of water
- 1 tsp. Himalayan sea salt

Directions:

1. Heat a grill over a medium heat. Coat the steak with a tbsp. of olive oil and season it with pepper. Allow the steak to grill for about 5-7 minutes for each side until the temperature shown by the thermometer reaches to 130 degrees. Remove the steak and allow it to rest for 5 minutes before slicing.
2. While steak is allowed to rest, toss the leeks with 1 tsp. of olive oil. Grill them over indirect heat, around the steak until

    they turn tender for about 6-7 minutes. Remove them and chop roughly.
3. Process arugula together with oregano, garlic, vinegar, oil, water and salt in a blender until it turns smooth. Distribute the steak, greens and leeks into 4 plates and drizzle each serving with the dressing.

**Nutrition information per serving:** 378 calories, 10g carbs, 35g protein and 30g fats.

# 11. Tempeh Bacon (Gluten-Free, Lectin-Free)

Are you on lectin-free diet??? Then you must try this easy lectin-free tempeh bacon recipe in a vegan BLT together with your favourite sweet potato hash!

Prep time: 5 mins
Cook time: 5 mins
Total time: 10 mins
**Yield:** 2-4 servings

Ingredients:

- 8 oz. thinly sliced grain-free tempeh
- 3 tbsps. of coconut aminos
- 1 tbsp. of olive oil
- 1 tbsp. of rice wine vinegar
- ¼ tsp. of sea salt
- 1 tsp. of smoked paprika
- ¼ tsp. of freshly ground black pepper
- 5 drops of liquid stevia
- ¼ tsp liquid smoke
- Pinch of cayenne
- 2 tbsps. of coconut oil

Directions:

1. Mix all the ingredients except tempeh and coconut oil in a shallow dish.
2. Add tempeh slices and turn to coat and marinate for 5 minutes.
3. Add 1 tbsp. of coconut oil in a pan by heating to medium high heat.

4. Reduce the heat down to medium and add the tempeh slices after 5 minutes of marinating.
5. Cook for 2-4 minutes by flipping occasionally from each side.
6. Pour in the coconut oil in the pan if required. If left with extra marinade in the pan, reduce the heat and spoon the extra marinade on top of the slices while cooking.

**Nutritional information per serving:** 175 calories, 17g carbs, 12g protein and 25g fats.

## 12. Large Cassava Tortillas (Grain-Free, Vegan, & Lectin-Free)

Very easy to make these lectin free tortillas! Require only 6 ingredients and can be made within 20 minutes.

**Total time: 20 minutes**

**Yield:** 3 servings

Ingredients:

- 1 ½ cup (192 g) cassava flour + extra for rolling
- ¾ cup (6.5 oz.) + 1 tbsp. water
- 2 tbsp. (1 oz.) olive oil
- 1 tsp. xanthan gum
- ½ tsp. salt
- ¼ tsp. baking soda

Directions:

1. Take a medium bowl and combine all of the ingredients and mix well using a wooden spoon until the dough begins to form.
2. When it gets thick, use your hands to knead the dough until all the flour is fully incorporated and the dough turns smooth.
3. The dough shouldn't be sticky yet it should be moist. If it's too sticky, add flour and if there's still some bits of flour then add water.
4. Make the dough into a log shape and divide it into three equal pieces.
5. Take two large parchment sheets to roll. Place a sheet on to the counter and dust it with cassava flour.
6. Place one of the three pieces of dough on the sheet and dust it with more cassava flour, place the second sheet on the

top. Use a rolling pin to roll it out roughly up to 10-12 inches to make it thin.
7. By using your hands, mend the edges together then trim a circle with a knife.
8. Heat a skillet (12-14 inches) over medium heat. Grease it lightly with coconut oil or olive oil and place in one tortilla.
9. Serve warm and enjoy!

**Nutrition information per serving:** 136 calories, 30g carbs, 8g protein and 45 fats.

## 13. Roasted Cauliflower Rice

What can be much easier than this roasted cauliflower rice recipe? You just need to roast with addition of your favourite seasonings and top with scallions and fried eggs if desired.

Prep time: 5 mins
Cook time 25 mins
Total time 30 mins

Yield: 2 servings

Ingredients

- 1 head cauliflower, riced
- 2 tbsps. avocado oil
- 1 tsp. paprika
- ½ tsp. garlic powder
- ½ tsp. onion powder
- ¼ tsp. turmeric
- Sea salt and pepper, to taste
- Sliced scallions
- Sesame seeds
- Fried eggs (or tofu fried in pan for vegan option)
- **Sriracha**

Instructions

1. Preheat the oven to 425 degrees F. Meanwhile, prepare a rimmed baking sheet with parchment.
2. Add oil and transfer the riced cauliflower over the prepared baking sheet. Add the seasonings to taste. Stir well to combine.
3. Bake for about 12 minutes and then stir. Place the sheet back to oven and bake for 13 more minutes until golden and crispy. Keep an eye on the rice till the end to avoid burning.

4. Serve with toasted sesame seeds, sliced scallions and fried eggs or tofu with a drizzle of sriracha.

**Nutrition information per serving:** 105 Calories, 9g carbs, 13g protein and 15g fats.

# 14. Stir Fry Broccoli Cooked In Teriyaki Sauce Served With Cauliflower Rice (Vegan, Lectin-Free & Sugar-Free)

This lectin free and sugar free vegan recipe is perfect for your dinner! Ginger garlic Teriyaki sauce adds umami flavor to the broccoli.

**Total time:** 20 minutes

**Yield:** 2 servings

Ingredients:

- Broccoli head cut into florets and thinly sliced stems (1 large)
- 1 thinly cut carrot
- 3 medium chopped garlic cloves
- 2 thinly sliced scallions
- 2 tablespoon homemade teriyaki sauce
- 1 tablespoon sesame oil
- ¾ teaspoon toasted sesame seeds
- Salt to taste
- A pinch of cinnamon powder
- Lightly ground black pepper
- 12 oz. of cauliflower rice for serving
- Extra teriyaki sauce for serving
- Fresh cilantro for serving

Directions:

1. Place a large pan over medium high heat. Once hot, pour in toasted sesame oil and allow it to simmer. Add carrot, broccoli, and salt to taste.
2. Cook for about 8 minutes by constant stirring until the veggies turn tender.

3. Meanwhile, cook cauliflower rice as per the directions given on the package. Cook the cauliflower rice with addition of some coconut oil and salt until tender for about 6 minutes.
4. After the vegetables turn lightly tender, add garlic and a pinch of cinnamon powder and ground black pepper and cook for 2 more minutes.
5. Pour in teriyaki sauce and add chopped scallions. Mix well to combine.
6. Serve broccoli with cauliflower rice and some extra teriyaki sauce. You can give a touch of fresh cilantro as well.

**Nutrition information per serving:** 226 calories, 35 g carbs, 12g protein and 30g fats.

# 15. Lectin-Free Vegan Pumpkin Spice Cauliflower Rice Soup

Try this one pot meal of lectin-free vegan pumpkin spice cauliflower soup that can be cooked in only 15 minutes.

Prep time: 5 mins
Cook time: 10 mins
Total time: 15 mins

**Yield:** 4 cups

Ingredients:

- 4 cups organic cauliflower rice
- ½ cup diced organic red onion
- 1 freshly crushed garlic clove
- 2 tbsps. organic extra-virgin olive oil
- 2 tsps. organic pumpkin spice
- 1 tsp. organic dried rosemary
- ½ - 1 tsp. Himalayan pink salt
- ½ tsp. freshly ground black pepper
- 1 can full-fat coconut milk

Directions:
1. Add olive oil to the skillet and allow it to simmer. Add onions, garlic, rosemary, Himalayan salt, pepper and sauté for about 2-3 minutes over medium heat.
2. Add in the cauliflower rice, pumpkin spice and full can of coconut milk to the skillet and mix well. Add seasonings according to your taste.
3. Allow cauliflower rice to simmer on low-medium heat until thawed and soften, if using frozen cauliflower rice.

4. Give it a finishing touch with extra dried rosemary and freshly ground black pepper.
5. Serve it warm.
6. **Enjoy!**

**Nutrition information per serving:** 98 calories, 12g carbs, 6g protein and 5.5g fats.

# Conclusion

We always wanted to look good and to feel good. When we go up and become an adult, we get more conscious on how we look like. We try different types of dieting methods. We follow fads and trends here and there. We compete with our friends and colleagues and even to ourselves just to get the right body we wanted. We see everything on TV, we hear the news about the how people lose weight and we encounter these products to lose weights. Most of them do not really work. While everyone still struggles on the process of dieting, this article has already given the basic secrets to successful lose weight dieting.

Some people may already have started but for those are still on the verge of deciding whether to try it out, be confident that you will get better results. It is recommended that you not only eat good food but you enjoy them at the same time. We also emphasize that you should learn the habit of eating delicious food as it becomes easier to lose weight.

Weight control methods can be successful if lose weight dieting is maintained without compromising overall health. When you get successful in weight reduction program, you also promote permanent life-style changes. The physical and psychological benefits of maintaining the right weight can be observed when it is done are the right way. It is, however, more beneficial when you personalize the weight reduction plan based on individual's needs and lifestyle.

When you get the right ingredients of lose weight dieting like exercise and sleep, you tend to get the weight you desire. We know that getting the right weight also prevents us from certain diseases. Not only that, we function well in our daily workload. We become successful when we do our job right.

For all of us, it is definitely important that we look good. By getting the proper nutrition and understanding how the body works, we get the optimum level of health and it gives you the glow you deserve. Sometimes, we just overlooked at the secrets of getting the best of us. We miss to identify how we get through with getting healthy and looking good. Therefore, being conscious about our weight and our physical appearance is not bad at all. It actually reflects on how we live our lives and how we become effective creatures. Being healthy gives you an overall functionality,

# Part 2

# Introduction

Developing a healthy lifestyle is very high on everyone's agenda in this day and age. But a healthy lifestyle needs to be accompanied by developing healthy eating habits that are not strict, harmful or restrictive. Most diets however, are all of those things. There is always a new 'it' diet which swoops the nation, but how do you differentiate the good from the bad diets when cooking for your family?

In this book I want to discuss the pro's and con's of a Lectin-free diet. How it works, what are the benefits of going Lectin-free and how it can improve your and your family's health. I will also share with you 70 of my favorite healthy, simple and delicious Lectin-free family friendly recipes for every occasion.

So, lets dive straight in….

**What are Lectins?**

Lectins are a special type of protein which exist in large amounts in many types of foods like beans, nuts and grains. Scientists and nutritionists have been researching lectins for years and have found that lectins may impact your health in multiple ways. Lectins are categorized as anti-nutrients because they block the absorption of certain nutrients.

In The Plant Paradox, Dr. Grundy notes that lectins are particularly harmful because this specific protein was developed by plants as a defense mechanism against predators such as animals and insects. He also notes that eating lectin containing foods may cause a 'leaky gut' therefore allow bacteria to penetrate your bloodstream and may severely damage cells and cause digestive problems and deficiencies. Dr. Grundy also believes that lectins are directly linked with unexplained weight gain, inflammation, autoimmune diseases and diabetes.

# Chapter 1: Nutrient Absorption

Nutrients in our diets are largely absorbed in the small intestine. The small intestine is approximately 5 feet long which increases the surface area and ultimately the absorptive capacity of nutrients.

When lectins are consumed and adhere to the intestinal wall, the surface area of nutrient absorption is reduced. Nutrient deficiencies can lead to serious symptoms including: anemia, osteoporosis, neuropathy (nerve dysfunction), alopecia (hair loss), malnutrition, and increased susceptibility to infections.

Lectins can also negatively impact the gut bacteria which is necessary for proper immune system function and vitamin synthesis. Gut bacteria also aid in the absorption of certain minerals such as calcium, iron, and magnesium. Reducing lectin intake can dramatically enhance nutrient absorption in those suffering from lectin induced malabsorptive issues.

**5 Ways to Improve Nutrient Absorption:**

**Avoiding alcohol during meals**

Drinking alcohol during meals disrupts absorption of some nutrients.

**Chewing your food well**

Digestion starts in the mouth, with the help of enzymes in your saliva. Chewing helps the breakdown of food, so it reaches the stomach already pre-digested.

**Taking probiotics**

Look after the friendly bacteria in your digestive system because it is instrumental in breaking down your food and allowing your body to use the nutrients. Take probiotics either as supplements or by including fermented food in your diet, e.g. yogurt, sauerkraut.

**Food combining**

According to the food synergy principle, when certain foods are combined, they become much healthier than when consumed individually, e.g.: broccoli and tomato, avocado and tomato, honey and walnuts.

**Adding fat to veggies, rather than cooking them in fat**

Fat is necessary because it's a major fuel source, but also because it helps you absorb certain nutrients, such as fat-soluble vitamins A, D, E and K. However, cooking in fat increases calorie intake, so the recommended way of getting the most from both good fats and vegetables, is to add fats/oil to vegetables (raw or cooked) just before serving them.

# Chapter 2: Methods To Reduce Lectin Content

As discussed earlier, there are many foods that contain high amounts of lectins. However, there are steps that can be taken to significantly reduce lectin levels of certain foods.

I have found that using a pressure cooker instant pot can effectively reduce the amount of lectins in most of the high-lectin foods. The moist heat in the pressure cooker is beneficial to reducing lectin levels.

Although you might think that the same rule would apply to using a slow cooker, unfortunately this is not the case. The temperature in a slow cooker does not reach a high enough level to effectively eliminate lectins.

Other known methods of reducing lectin levels include: fermenting, boiling, sprouting, peeling and deseeding.

Grains and legumes can also be soaked, preferably in a baking soda bath overnight. The soak water should be replaced multiple times to ensure adequate disposal of the lectins that have leeched into the water.

**Foods Allowed**

The following foods contain very little or no lectins and are therefore advised to consume regularly.

- Eggs (pasture-raised)
- Fruits: mango, citrus, pineapple, blueberries, apples
- Onions
- Mushrooms

- Sweet potatoes
- Celery
- Brewers or nutritional yeast
- Raw honey
- Extra virgin olive oil
- Avocado oil
- Hemp protein
- Fish (wild caught)
- Beef (grass fed)
- Chicken
- Coconut flour
- Pork
- Liver
- Bone broth
- Leafy greens (spinach, bok choy, etc.)
- Cruciferous Vegetables (broccoli, brussel sprouts)
- Ghee (clarified butter)
- Dark Chocolate (72% less Cacao)
- Stevia

**Foods to Avoid**

The following food items contain higher amounts of lectins and should be limited or avoided. The food preparation methods listed previously in this book can significantly reduce lectin levels.

- Grains (wheat, barley, rye, oats, ancient grains, pasta, bread, corn)
- Dairy products (cheese, milk, yoghurt, cream, butter)

- Fruits and vegetables (squash, zucchini, pumpkin, potatoes, eggplants, peppers, tomatoes, melons)
- Tree nuts
- Legumes (beans, lentils, peas, chickpeas and peanuts)
- Yeast (except brewer and nutritional)
- Sugar, maple syrup

# Chapter 3: Benefits And Possible Risks Of Lectin-Free Diet

Before embarking on the Lectin-free diet journey, I think it is important to note some of the benefits as well as the risks that are associated with this diet.

**Benefits**

- Some scientists believe that lectins are considerably harmful for your health and are linked to inflammation. They are also considered to be linked to autoimmune diseases like diabetes, rheumatoid arthritis and even celiac disease. With the Lectin-free diet, you can avoid damaging your health by decreasing your lectin intake.

- Inflammation for an extended period of time has been proven to cause serious medical issues like cancer, depression and even cardiac complications. Eliminating lectins from your diet can potentially lower your risk of obtaining these illnesses.

- Lectins are not digestible and bind to the cell membranes lining in your digestive track. This means that lectin build up has the potential of causing damage and disrupting your metabolism.

-

**Risks**

With numerous benefits, the Lectin-free diet also brings along some risks.

- It is a restrictive plan and can be hard to follow for a longer time period.

- It removes or limits certain nutritious foods like beans, whole grains and even some vegetables.
- May be expensive and hard to tackle financially because of the inclusion of pasture raised meats, highly priced supplements and special milks.

According to medical and scientific research, the consumption of whole grains can be beneficial in reducing the risk of cardiac diseases, cancer and even diabetes. There are many health benefits of fruits and vegetable consumption. Their high consumption may reduce the dangers of various medical complications including cardiac issues, lungs related medical issues and even considerable weight loss alongside reducing the risk of cancer. The Lectin-free diet is considered to be hard to follow by vegans and vegetarians as legumes, seeds, nuts and whole grains are the source for plant-based protein. They are also the sources for provision of dietary fiber, which means there is a risk of constipation while consuming a Lectin-free diet because of the lower intake of dietary fibers.

# Chapter 4: Basic Healthy Eating Guidelines

### Stop eating before you feel full

If you eat slowly, you'll find it easy to know when you've had enough. Conversely, if you eat until you feel full, it is considered that you have over-eaten.

### Learn healthy cooking methods

As a rule of thumb, stir-fried and steamed vegetables are the healthiest way to cook. This way of cooking is also very convenient because it's easy and quick.

### Adopt a healthy diet

There are many ways to eat healthily, so go for a diet which supports your lifestyle, and which consists of ingredients available locally.

### Eat in tune with the seasons

Choosing seasonal and locally produced food is the easiest way to ensure you eat fresh and naturally ripened fruit and vegetable. For example, poultry from your local butcher theoretically will be better than poultry found at your local grocery store.

### Enjoy your food

Never eat something you don't like. Food which you, for whatever reason, find disgusting, isn't nourishing. Your body is smart and knows what's best for you. There is a reason it reacts differently to certain foods - rather than force yourself to eat something just because it's supposed to be good for you, learn to listen to the subtle signs your body sends.

**Stop obsessing about nutritional value of each meal**

This kills both the joy of cooking, as well as the joy of eating. Instead, learn to recognize the quality of food the way Orientals do: learn how certain foods affect your metabolism or your dosha.

**Stop feeling guilty**

Allow yourself to eat according to the 80/20 principle: eating healthy 80% of the time and treating yourself occasionally to something unhealthy (i.e. chocolate, pizza, etc.). This method creates sanity, and instead of losing your mind for going 'off' diet, learn to implement foods which you enjoy throughout your day.

**Healthy snacks**

If you like eating between meals, always keep some fresh fruit or packs of dried fruit, nuts and seeds in your car, desk or bag) – this stops you going to the shop and picking up a chocolate bar or any other bad snacks!

**Water, water, water!**

Arguably the most important! Don't forget to drink water throughout the day. Drink at least 2 liters per day. The body is 70% water, why wouldn't you give it the fuel it needs!

**Healthy doesn't have to mean tasteless**

Find ways to bring even simple meals to life. With so many different kinds of natural spices to choose from, even a very restrictive diet's taste and appearance can be improved with a little bit of imagination. Learn to cook creatively.

**Don't keep unhealthy food at home.**

Quite obvious, but its something that most people overlook. Have you noticed, that when you go shopping and you never buy any 'treats' then you don't really crave them, as you know they inaccessible. A great trick for you guys!

# Chapter 5: Advantages Of Using An Instant Pot Electric Pressure Cooker

You may be coming to the Instant Pot with preconceived notions of what it actually is. Maybe you've heard stories that they can overflow or spray food everywhere, or maybe you remember the old-fashioned pressure cookers that loudly (and annoyingly) whistled.

Forget all those ideas, because the Instant Pot is different. Because the Instant Pot is an electric pressure cooker that was specifically designed to be safer than stovetop pressure cookers, it has few of the issues of the old-fashioned pressure cookers. But if you're like me and like to know how things work, you might be wondering how, exactly, the Instant Pot cooks food using the pressure cooking setting.

The Instant Pot electric pressure cooker program begins when you set the Pressure Release valve to "Sealing." From there, you select the program and set the desired time. The Instant Pot will give you 30-60 seconds to make your selections, then it will automatically initiate the program.

As the Instant Pot begins to build heat, the pressure increases in the pot and the boiling point of the water or liquid in the pot also increases. As more and more steam is generated, the pressure continues to increase inside the pot. The water begins to reach a very high temperature, yet the high pressure and the increased boiling point prevents the water from boiling or evaporating.

The high-heat, high-moisture environment of the Instant Pot means you get exceptionally quick cooking times and incredibly moist food. Even typically dry cuts of meat, such as boneless skinless chicken breasts come out juicy and moist in just a few minutes. This makes it almost impossible to overcook or dry out your food—and who doesn't want that?!

**Inside Your Instant Pot Pressure Cooker**

While other electric pressure cookers may have features that are different from the Instant Pot, almost all electric pressure cookers have several key parts:

**Push down pressure release:** The valves that are installed in the Instant Pot are designed with an innovative Anti-Block Shield that allows them to automatically react to changing conditions in the pot. The valves remain locked until the pressure goes beyond the specified threshold, at which point the valve pushes itself upward, slowly releasing the pressure and returning it to normal levels. These release valves are intelligently controlled with electronic sensors which automatically alter the settings depending on the type of food you're cooking.

**Locking mechanism:** The Instant Pot has a sealing ring that creates a completely airtight chamber inside the pot so that steam can build up. Once you turn the pot lid to the closed position, the vacuum seal is formed. The lid locks in place, so that you can't accidentally open the lid when the pot is at a high pressure.

**Inner pot:** Sometimes also referred to as the cooking pot. The inner pot is stainless steel, so it's easy to wash and can also be used to store leftovers in the refrigerator.

**Heating element:** The heating element is electric, meaning that you can plug in the pot and set it on your countertop, just like a slow cooker. This makes it perfect for small kitchens!

**Sensors:** The Instant Pot has several built-in pressure and temperature sensors that make it safer than a nonelectric pressure cooker. These sensors monitor the internal environment, maintain the desired cooking conditions, and help protect you from possible mishaps.

# Chapter 6: Breakfast Recipes

## Hard Boiled Eggs

(Total Time: 6 Min|Serves: 2)

**Ingredients:**
- 4 large pastured eggs
- 1 cup water

**Instructions:**
1. In the inner pot of the electric pressure cooker put in some water and then place a trivet in it.
2. Next, put the eggs over the trivet and then close the lid of the cooker along with closing the vent valve.
3. Select "Manual" and set the pressure on high for 5 minutes for the eggs to cook fully hard.
4. After the timer goes off, release the pressure naturally and open the lid of the cooker.

5. Take the eggs out and place them in the bowl of cold water.
6. Peel them and enjoy eating!

**Nutrition information:**
Calories 140
Total Fat 9 g
Carbs 2 g
Protein 12 g

# Egg Muffins

(Total Time: 25 Min | Serves: 4)

## Ingredients:
- 4 large pastured eggs
- ¼ teaspoon lemon pepper seasoning
- 1 green onion, diced
- 4 rashers of grass-fed bacon, precooked

## Instructions:
1. Add 1½ cups water and place the rack in the cooker pot.
2. In a mixing bowl, break eggs and whisk well. Add all the other ingredients and divide the muffin batter equally in muffin mounds.
3. Place the muffins on the rack or metal trivet. Cook on high pressure for 8 minutes.
4. Do a natural pressure release and remove the cooked muffins carefully.

## Nutrition information:
Calories 141
Fat 11 g;
Carbs 2.2 g
Protein 9.3 g

# Crust Free Broccoli And Ham Quiche

(Total Time: 40 Min | Serves: 4)

**Ingredients:**
- 6 whole pastured eggs
- 2 teaspoons of ghee
- ½ a cup ham, diced
- ½ a cup of broccoli florets, chopped
- 1 whole green onion, chopped
- ¼ teaspoon of salt
- Pepper as needed

**Instructions:**
1. Place a trivet in the bottom of your Pot.
2. Add a cup of water.
3. Take an oven safe 1-quart round dish and grease with 1 teaspoon of ghee.
4. Take a medium bowl and add eggs, beat them.
5. Add the remaining teaspoon of ghee, ham, green onion, broccoli, pepper and salt.
6. Stir all ingredients together.
7. Pour the mix into the dish.
8. Cover the dish with aluminum foil.
9. Transfer the dish into your trivet using a sling.
10. Lock up the lid and cook on high pressure for 30 minutes.
11. Release the pressure naturally over 10 minutes.

**Nutrition information:**
Calories: 354
Fat: 23g
Carbs: 25g
Protein: 13g

# Vanilla Muffin

(Total Time: 14 Min | Serves: 2)

**Ingredients:**
- 2 large pastured eggs
- 4 tablespoons extra virgin olive oil
- 4 teaspoons granular monk, fruit sweetener
- 2 tablespoons coconut flour
- 2 tablespoons seasonal fruit
- 2 tablespoons tigernut flour
- 1 teaspoon baking powder
- 1 teaspoon vanilla extract
- ¼ teaspoon sea salt

**Instructions:**
1. Take a bowl and mix in olive oil along with coconut flour, tigernut flour, sweetener, baking powder, vanilla extract, and salt.
2. Next, add in the egg and beat with a fork until batter is silky smooth.
3. Now, gently fold in the fruits of your choice.
4. Transfer the mixture into a mini bread loaf pan.
5. Place a steam basket in the pressure cooker and add in 2 cups of water in it.
6. Carefully place the mini loaf pan straight without tilting.
7. Close the lid and turn the heat to high and when it reaches pressure, turn the flame to minimum and cook for 12 minutes.
8. Pressure release naturally and use a toothpick to check whether the muffin is cooked or not; if the toothpick comes out clean, then the muffin is done.
9. Serve warm or cold as per your choice.

**Nutrition information:**
Calories 347
Fat 32.6 g
Carbs 10.2 g
Protein 6.2 g

# Glory Muffins

(Total Time: 50 Min | Serves: 6)

**Ingredients:**
- 1 cup sweet potato, cooked and mashed
- 1 cup raisins
- 1 cup walnuts, chopped
- ½ cup raw honey
- 2 teaspoons cinnamon
- 4 pastured eggs
- 1 cup coconut, shredded
- ¼ cup carrot, shredded
- 1 ½ cup almond flour
- 2 teaspoons vanilla extract
- 2 teaspoons baking powder

**Instructions:**
1. Take a bowl and mix in all the ingredients of the glory muffins.
2. Take a medium muffin tray and grease it using cooking spray.
3. Divide the batter among the cups.
4. Take a pressure cooker and set a trivet in it.
5. Place the muffin mound over the trivet making sure that it does not tilt.
6. Close the lid of the pressure cooker and allow it to cook for about 30 minutes.
7. After the timer goes off, allow the pressure to release naturally and then remove the lid.
8. Use a toothpick to check whether the muffin is cooked or not; if the toothpick comes out clean, then the muffin is done.
9. Transfer the tray onto the table and allow the muffins to cool down.

10. Finally, release the muffins from the tray and serve.

**Nutrition information:**
Calories 460
Fat 23.4 g
Carbs 38.4 g
Protein 8.4 g

# Picatta Potatoes

(Total Time: 13 Min | Serves: 4)

### Ingredients:
- 2 cups of water
- 4 russet potatoes, sliced
- 2 tablespoons of coconut oil
- 1 whole onion, julienned
- A quarter cup of vegetable broth
- 2 tablespoons of fresh lemon juice
- ¼ of cup of parsley
- Salt as needed
- Pepper as needed

### Instructions:
1. Add water to the pot and add potatoes.
2. Lock up the lid and cook on high pressure for 5 minutes.
3. Release the pressure naturally.
4. Drain the potatoes into a colander.
5. Add coconut oil to the pot and allow it to heat up in Sauté mode.
6. Add potatoes, lemon juice and broth.
7. Sauté for 5 minutes and remove the heat.
8. Add parsley and season with salt and pepper.

### Nutrition information:
Calories: 442
Fat: 19g
Carbohydrates: 30g
Protein: 33g

# Ginger Bread

(Total Time: 7 Min | Serves: 2)

**Ingredients:**
- 1 teaspoon ginger, grounded
- ½ teaspoon cinnamon
- ¼ teaspoon cloves
- 2 tablespoons butter, softened
- ¼ teaspoon nutmeg
- 4 teaspoons maple flavored erythritol syrup
- 1 teaspoon apple cider vinegar
- 1 tablespoon water
- 2 tablespoons coconut flour
- 2 tablespoons cassava flour
- 1 teaspoon baking powder
- large eggs, lightly beaten

**Instructions:**
1. Take a bowl and add in the butter along with ginger, cinnamon, coconut flour, baking powder, cassava flour, and spices.
2. Next, in the same bowl combine in the syrup with cider vinegar; water, and egg.
3. Continue beating it briskly with a fork until batter is silky and steady.
4. Transfer the mixture into a mini bread loaf pan.
5. Place a steam basket in the pressure cooker and add in 2 cups of water in it.
6. Carefully place the mini loaf pan straight without tilting.
7. Close the lid and turn the heat to high and when it reaches pressure, turn the flame to minimum and cook for 6-8 minutes.

8. Pressure release naturally and use a toothpick to check whether the bread is cooked or not; if the toothpick comes out clean, then bread is done.
9. Serve hot.

**Nutrition information:**
Calories 215
Fat 16.2 g
Carbs 24.2 g
Protein 5.5 g

# Almond Flour Biscuits

(Total Time: 25 Min | Serves: 8)

**Ingredients:**
- 3 cups almond flour, blanched
- 2 teaspoons baking powder
- 1 teaspoon kosher salt
- 6 tablespoons cold butter, diced
- 6 tablespoons coconut cream
- 2 pastured eggs

**Instructions:**
1. In a bowl, mix together almond flour with salt and baking powder.
2. Next, take some cold diced butter and mix it with the flour.
3. Keep on cutting the butter and mixing in the flour till the dough is crumbly.
4. Make a hole in the center of the bowl and put in the eggs and cream together; mix both of the ingredients lightly with hands.
5. Next, incorporate the egg cream mixture with the rest of the flour and mix until soft dough is formed.
6. Make balls out of the cookie dough and then make cookies out of each ball. Make sure not to flatten the dough.
7. Grease a baking tray and put the cookies over it.
8. Place a trivet in the pressure cooker.
9. Carefully place the baking tray the pressure cooker without tilting.
10. Close the lid and turn the heat to high and when it reaches pressure, turn the flame to minimum and cook for 20 minutes.
11. Pressure release naturally and see whether the cookies are cooked properly by seeing the sides of the cookies.
12. Serve warm or cold as per your choice.

**Nutrition information:**
Calories 159
Fat 15.6 g
Carbs 2.7 g
Protein 3 .2g

# Early Morning Artichokes

(Total Time: 25 Min|Serves: 4)

**Ingredients:**
- 2 medium sized artichokes
- 1 lemon sliced in half
- 2 tablespoon of mayo (Vegan)
- 1 teaspoon of Dijon mustard
- 1 pinch of paprika

**Instructions:**
1. Wash the artichokes fully and remove any damaged outer leaves.
2. Trim the spins and cut the topped edge.
3. Wipe the cut edges using half a lemon.
4. Slice the stem and keep it on the side.
5. Add a cup of water to your pot.
6. Add the trimmed-up parts into a steamer basket
7. Lower down the steamer basket inside and spritz lemon.
8. Lock up the lid and cook on high pressure for 10 minutes.
9. Once the timer is out, release the pressure naturally.
10. Take a bowl and mix 2 tablespoon of vegan mayo (recipe provided) and season with paprika.

**Nutrition information:**
Calories: 77
Fat: 5g
Carbohydrates: 0g
Protein: 2g

# Chapter 7: Main Dishes

## Salmon Cakes

(Total Time: 30 Min|Serves: 8)

**Ingredients:**
- 24 oz salmon, canned
- 4 teaspoons primal palate seafood seasoning
- ½ cup Vidalia onion, minced
- 6 pastured egg yolks
- 6 tablespoons organic palm oil, shortenings
- 2 teaspoons chives, for garnish
- 4 teaspoons parsley, for garnish
- 8 lemon wedges, for garnish

**Instructions:**
1. In a bowl take salmon along with egg yolks and seafood seasoning and combine them well.

2. Next, add in the minced onion and mix to combine all the ingredients.
3. Make small patties out of the mixture with 2-inch thickness each and set them on a baking tray or any heat proof tray.
4. Now, take an electric pressure cooker and place a trivet in it with almost 2-inch thickness.
5. Next, place the baking tray/ heat proof tray in the pressure cooker while closing the lid and setting the temperature on manual high for 15 minutes.
6. After the time goes off, quick release the pressure naturally and open the lid.
7. Transfer the patties onto a tray.
8. Take a skillet and put some palm oil shortenings in it over a medium-high stove.
9. Next, place the patties over it, turning the sides until golden brown.
10. Transfer them on a plate and serve them with the garnish of lemon wedges, parsley and chives.

**Nutrition information:**
Calories 248
 Fat 18.8 g
 Carbs 1.8 g
Protein 18.7

# Cucumber Salmon Bites

(Total Time: 20 Min | Serves: 4)

**Ingredients:**
- 2 wholes cucumbers, sliced in coins
- 2 whole salmon, frozen
- 4 tablespoons Greek style yoghurt, unsweetened
- 4 teaspoons Dijon Mustard
- 2 teaspoons seafood seasoning

**Instructions:**
1. Take a pressure cooker and place a steamer rack in.
2. Place the frozen salmons over the rack and pressure cook it for about 5 minutes while closing the lid selecting the manual button.
3. After the timer goes off depressurize the cooker naturally and take out the salmons after opening up the lid and allow it to cool on a rack.
4. Next, take a bowl and mix together salmon with yoghurt, mustard and seasoning. Take cucumber slices and place the mixture over it.
5. Serve and enjoy eating!

**Nutrition information:**
Calories 145
 Fat 5.7 g
 Carbs 5.8 g
Protein 16.2 g

# Salmon Bowls Asian Style

(Total Time: 45 Min | Serves: 4)

**Ingredients:**
- 2 cups celery, chopped
- ¼ teaspoon garlic
- ¼ teaspoon ginger
- ¼ teaspoon red pepper flakes
- 4 cups white mushrooms, thinly sliced
- 1 tablespoon extra virgin olive oil
- 1 ½ lb wild caught salmon, fillet
- ¼ teaspoon himalayan pink salt
- ½ teaspoon fish sauce
- 4 tablespoons coconut aminos
- 2 teaspoons sesame oil, toasted
- 4 tablespoons green onion, sliced
- 6 cups cauliflower, head only, grated
- ¼ teaspoon salt
- ¼ teaspoon pepper
- 2 tablespoons ghee

**Instructions:**
1. Marinate salmon with ginger, garlic, olive oil, and red pepper flakes; set aside.
2. Next, take a pressure cooker and place a steamer rack in it; place the salmon fillets on it.
3. Now, cover the pressure cooker with the lid to cook it on high pressure for about 25 minutes after selecting the manual button.
4. Meanwhile, place a wok on the stove over a medium high heat and put in the mushrooms along with celery and season them with salt and pepper; keep on frying.

5. Now add in the grated cauliflower head along with green onion, fish sauce, coconut amino, sesame oil, garlic powder and ginger.
6. When the timer goes off, depressurize the cooker naturally and take the salmon out and place it onto a cutting board.
7. Shred the salmon using two forks.
8. Transfer the salmon into the serving bowl along with the other ingredients and after tossing them all, enjoy!

**Nutrition information:**
Calories 351
Fat 20.3 g
Carbs 15.5 g
Protein 30 g

# Flavour Bomb Asian Brussels Sprouts

(Total Time: 8 Min | Serves: 4)

**Ingredients:**
- 3 tablespoons coconut aminos
- 1 tablespoon rice wine vinegar
- 2 tablespoons sesame oil
- 2 teaspoons garlic powder
- 1 teaspoon onion powder
- 1 tablespoon paprika
- ¼ teaspoon cayenne pepper
- 1 teaspoon salt
- 1 tablespoon chopped almonds
- 2 lbs. Brussels sprouts, halved

**Instructions:**
1. In a small bowl, combine the coconut aminos, rice wine vinegar, sesame oil, garlic powder, onion powder, paprika, cayenne pepper, and salt. Set aside.
2. Select the Sauté setting and add the almonds. Stir constantly until toasted, watching them carefully so they don't burn. Press Cancel to turn off the Sauté setting then add the reserved sauce to the pot. Add the brussels sprouts and stir well to coat them in the sauce.
3. Lock the lid and set the Pressure Release to Sealing. Select the Pressure Cook or Manual setting and set the cooking time to 3 minutes at high pressure.
4. Once the timer goes off, use a kitchen towel or oven mitts to protect your hand and move the Pressure Release knob to Venting to perform a quick pressure release.
5. Open the lid and taste, adding salt and pepper to taste, if necessary. Serve warm over cauliflower rice or as a side for a protein.

**Nutrition information:**
Calories: 368
 Fat: 18 g
Carbs: 12 g
Protein: 42 g

# Shrimps On Lettuce Leaves

(Total Time: 23 Min | Serves: 4)

## Ingredients:
- 1 teaspoon taco seasoning
- 24 whole raw shrimps, thawed, peeled and deveined
- 2 teaspoons extra virgin olive oil
- 2 cups romaine lettuce, shredded
- 1 whole radish, thinly sliced
- ½ avocado, diced
- ½ cup cilantro, chopped
- 1 whole roma tomato, diced, seedless
- 1 whole lime wedge for garnish
- 8 whole large lettuce leaves

## Instructions:
1. Marinate the shrimps with the olive oil and the taco seasoning.
2. Place the steamer rack inside the electric pressure cooker and place the shrimps on it.
3. Cover it with the lid and pressure cook it for 3 minutes on high heat.
4. Next, when the timer goes off depressurize the cooker naturally and remove the lid.
5. Carefully transfer the shrimps onto a cooling rack.
6. Next, in a bowl take, cilantro, diced tomatoes, and romaine lettuce.
7. Now assemble everything on the lettuce leaves and enjoy eating.

## Nutrition information:
Calories 174
Fat 8.5 g

Carbs 5.4 g
Protein 21 g

# Amazingly Adaptable Roasted Sweet Potatoes

(Total Time: 12 Min | Serves: 4)

**Ingredients:**
- ¼ cup olive oil or ghee
- 4 medium sweet potatoes, peeled or unpeeled, in 1-inch pieces
- 1 teaspoon garlic powder
- 1 teaspoon sea salt
- ¼ teaspoon pepper
- 1 cup chicken or vegetable broth

**Instructions:**
1. Select the Sauté setting on the Instant Pot and heat the olive oil or ghee. Add the sweet potatoes, salt, pepper, and garlic powder to the pot and sauté for 5 minutes, stirring constantly. Add the broth and stir well.
2. Press Cancel to reset the cooking method. Lock the lid and set the Pressure Release to Sealing. Select the Pressure Cook or Manual setting and set the cooking time to 7 minutes at high pressure.
3. Once the timer goes off, use a kitchen towel or oven mitts to protect your hand and move the Pressure Release knob to Venting to perform a quick pressure release.
4. Open the lid and taste, adding salt and pepper to taste, if necessary. Serve warm over a salad or as a side for chicken or another protein.

**Nutrition information:**
Calories: 265
Fat: 16 g
Carbs: 18 g
Protein: 20 g

# Southern Stewed Greens

(Total Time: 15 Min|Serves: 4)

**Ingredients:**
- ¼ lb. bacon, in 1-inch pieces (omit to make this dish vegetarian)
- 5 cloves garlic, roughly chopped
- 2 large bunches kale, collard greens, or chard, de-stemmed and roughly chopped
- 3/4 cup chicken or vegetable broth
- Salt to taste
- Pepper to taste
- Optional: 1 tablespoon apple cider vinegar

**Instructions:**
1. Select the Sauté setting and add the bacon, cooking until it has rendered its fat and crisped up, 5-7 minutes. Add the garlic and cook, stirring constantly, for 1 minute. Add the greens, broth, and salt and pepper to taste. You may need to add the greens in batches, stir, and allow to wilt slightly until it all fits in the pot.
2. Press Cancel to reset the cooking method. Lock the lid and set the Pressure Release to Sealing. Select the Pressure Cook or Manual setting and set the cooking time to 5 minutes at high pressure.
3. Once the timer goes off, use a kitchen towel or oven mitts to protect your hand and move the Pressure Release knob to Venting to perform a quick pressure release.
4. Open the lid, taste, and add more salt and pepper if necessary. If desired, stir in 1 tablespoon of apple cider vinegar to add brightness to the dish. Serve warm.

**Nutrition information:**
Calories: 368
Fat: 18 g
Carbs: 12 g
Protein: 42 g

# Balsamic And Garlic Stewed Kale

(Total Time: 9 Min | Serves: 4)

## Ingredients:
- 1 tablespoon olive oil
- 5 cloves garlic, roughly chopped
- 2 large bunches kale, de-stemmed and roughly chopped
- 1 cup chicken broth
- Salt to taste
- Pepper to taste
- 3 tablespoons balsamic vinegar

## Instructions:
1. Select the Sauté setting and heat the olive oil. Add the garlic and cook, stirring constantly, until fragrant, 3-5 minutes. Add the kale, broth, and salt and pepper to taste.
2. Press Cancel to reset the cooking method. Lock the lid and set the Pressure Release to Sealing. Select the Pressure Cook or Manual setting and set the cooking time to 4 minutes at high pressure.
3. Once the timer goes off, use a kitchen towel or oven mitts to protect your hand and move the Pressure Release knob to Venting to perform a quick pressure release.
4. Open the lid and add the balsamic vinegar. Taste and add more salt and pepper if necessary. Serve warm.

## Nutrition information:
Calories: 195
Fat: 19 g
Carbs: 3 g
Protein: 3 g

# Shrimp Tacos With Pomegranate Salsa

(Total Time: 40 Min | Serves: 4)

### Ingredients:
- 1 lb raw shrimp, large, peeled and deveined
- 1 teaspoon jerk seasoning
- 1 tablespoon extra virgin olive oil
- 1 cup vine ripened tomato, seedless, diced
- 2/3 cup mango, peeled, and diced
- 2 tablespoons red onion, finely diced
- 1/3 cup pomegranate seeds
- 1 tablespoon lime juice
- ¼ teaspoon salt
- ¼ teaspoon cilantro
- 2 cups romaine lettuce, shredded
- 4 cassava flour tortillas

### Instructions:
1. Season the shrimps with the jerk seasoning and set aside.
2. Place a steamer rack in the electric pressure cooker and pressure cook the shrimps in it for 3 minutes while covering it with lid.
3. Next, after the timer goes off, depressurize the cooker naturally and open the lid.
4. Transfer the shrimps onto a cooling rack.
5. Next, take a mixing bowl and place the pomegranate seeds, mango, tomato, and red onion in it along with drizzle of olive oil, lime juice, salt and chopped cilantro.
6. Warm the tortillas over the burner and assemble the tacos by placing the shrimps over the tortillas along with the pomegranate salsa.

### Nutrition information:

Calories 263
Fat 6.4 g
Carbs 23.5 g
Protein 28.3 g

# Salmon Salad With Avocado Salsa

(Total Time: 30 Min | Serves: 4)

**Ingredients:**
- ¼ teaspoon sea salt
- 3 tablespoons green onion, sliced
- 1 ½ teaspoon jalapeno pepper, raw, seeded and minced
- 1 lb(4 fillets) wild salmon filet
- 1 teaspoon extra virgin olive oil
- 1 teaspoon adobo seasoning
- 1 whole avocado, diced
- ¼ cup cilantro, minced
- ½ lime, juice
- 1/8 teaspoon black pepper, freshly grounded

**Instructions:**
1. Marinate the salmon with the olive oil and adobo seasoning and set aside.
2. Take a pressure cooker and place a steamer rack in it.
3. Next, place the salmon fillets over the rack and allow it to cook for 5 minutes under pressure by closing the lid of the electric pressure cooker.
4. After the time goes off, depressurize the cooker naturally and remove the lid from the top.
5. Now, take out the salmon fillets and place them on a cooling rack.
6. Take a bowl and combine together the avocado, lime juice, cilantro, sliced green onion, and jalapeno pepper, salt and freshly grounded pepper; set aside.
7. Place the salmon fillets on the serving plate and all the mixed greens over the top and enjoy eating.

**Nutrition information:**

Calories 220
Fat 12.9 g
Carbs 3.3 g
Protein 24.9 g

# Cod With Citrus And Fennel Salad

(Total Time: 20 Min | Serves: 2)

**Ingredients:**
- 2 cod fillets
- 1 lemon juice
- 1 tablespoon red wine vinegar
- 1 tablespoon extra-virgin olive oil
- 1 garlic clove, crushed
- 1 teaspoon Dijon mustard
- 1 red onion, julienned
- ½ bulb fennel, julienned
- 1 orange, small, fragments
- 2 cups baby spinach, rinsed thoroughly
- 1 cup pistachios, shelled
- 2 tablespoons orange zest

**Instructions:**
1. Season the cod with salt and set aside.
2. Next, take the electric pressure cooker and place a trivet inside it.
3. Place the cod over the steamer rack and pressure cook it for 15 minutes.
4. After the timer goes off, quick release the pressure naturally and open the lid.
5. Transfer the cod onto the plate and set aside.
6. In a bowl add in the lemon juice with red wine vinegar, extra virgin olive oil, garlic clove, and Dijon mustard; mix and set aside.
7. Next, in another bowl add in the red onion along with fennel, orange fragments, baby spinach, pistachios and orange zest.

8. Mix together the spinach with the dressing until the salad is evenly coated and serve onto the serving platter over the salmon fillets.

**Nutrition information:**
Calories 417
Fat 22.7 g
Carbs 32 g
Protein 29.6 g

# Perfect Cauliflower Mash

(Total Time: 10 Min | Serves: 4)

**Ingredients:**
- 1 large head cauliflower, cored and cut in large florets
- 1 cup chicken or vegetable broth
- 4 tablespoons ghee
- ½ tablespoon garlic powder
- Salt to taste
- Pepper to taste

**Instructions:**
1. Add the cauliflower and broth to the Instant Pot. Lock the lid and set the Pressure Release to Sealing. Select the Pressure Cook or Manual setting and set the cooking time to 5 minutes at high pressure.
2. Once the timer goes off, use a kitchen towel or oven mitts to protect your hand and move the Pressure Release knob to Venting to perform a quick pressure release.
3. Drain, reserving any excess broth, and return the cauliflower to the pot. With a potato masher, immersion blender, or fork, mash to your desired consistency, adding broth as needed for more moisture. Stir in the ghee and garlic powder, and add salt and pepper to taste.

**Nutrition information:**
Calories: 231
Fat: 20 g
Carbs: 5.5 g
Protein: 9 g

# Chicken And Goat Cheese Enchiladas

(Total Time: 50 Min | Serves: 4)

**Ingredients:**
- 1 tablespoon olive oil
- 4 ounces shiitake mushrooms, chopped
- 1/2 white onion, chopped
- 4 ounces pastured chicken, shredded
- 1 cup broth, divided
- ¼ teaspoon sea salt
- ¼ teaspoon black pepper
- 4 ounces goat cheese, crumbled
- 2 cloves garlic, peeled
- 1 ½ teaspoon apple cider vinegar
- ½ teaspoon coconut amino
- ½ teaspoon granular sweetener
- ¼ teaspoon cumin, grounded
- ¼ teaspoon oregano, dried
- 1/8 teaspoon paprika
- 4 cassava flour tortillas, warmed
- ½ cup cilantro, chopped

**Instructions:**
1. Take an electric pressure cooker and put 1 tablespoon of olive oil and onion in it after setting the cooker on Sauté mode.
2. Next, add in the mushrooms and cook for 1 minute.
3. Add chicken and give it a toss for 3 minutes.
4. Now, add in the chicken broth while closing the lid of the pressure cooker for 5 minutes.
5. After the timer goes off, depressurize the cooker naturally and open the lid.

6. Set the cooker on slow cook mode and add in half of the goat cheese; mix till dissolved; set aside.
7. For adobo sauce take a blender and add in the remaining broth with the garlic, vinegar, coconut amino, salt, sweetener, cumin, oregano and paprika.
8. Now take a flat baking sheet and put half of the adobo sauce on the base.
9. Next, take each tortilla and put in a dollop of mushroom and chicken mixture; roll and place it in the baking dish.
10. Now put the remaining adobo sauce and goat cheese over it and bake till bubble start to form and cheese melt.
11. Serve hot.

**Nutrition information:**
Calories 410
Fat 18.6 g
Carbs 31 g
Protein 29.1 g

# Steamed Cod With Herbs And Lemon

(Total Time: 40 Min|Serves: 4)

**Ingredients:**
- ¼ teaspoon salt
- ¼ teaspoon pepper
- 2 tablespoons extra virgin olive oil
- 4 garlic cloves, minced
- 4 tablespoons clarified butter
- 16 oz cod, wild, two whole filets
- 2 lemon, juice only
- ½ cup parsley, chopped

**Instructions:**
1. Season the cod with salt and set aside.
2. Put some ghee in the electric pressure cooker and alongside with some olive oil and some onions and select the Sauté mode for 4 minutes.
3. Add in the garlic and lemon juice and cook it further for 4 minutes.
4. Place a steamer rack in the electric pressure cooker and place the fillets over it and cook it on high pressure for about 5 minutes.
5. After the timer goes off, quick release the pressure and open the lid.
6. Transfer the cooked cod along with the sauce in a serving platter topped up with chopped parsley and lemon wedges.

**Nutrition information:**
Calories 297
Fat 19.7 g
Carbs 4.3 g
Protein 26.8 g

# 10-Minute Balsamic Roasted Beets

(Total Time: 11 Min | Serves: 6)

**Ingredients:**
- 6 medium beets, unpeeled
- 3 tablespoons balsamic vinegar
- 2 tablespoons olive oil
- Salt to taste
- Pepper to taste

**Instructions:**
1. Wash the beets well and remove any leaves. Add 1 cup of water to the Instant Pot and place the trivet on top. Arrange the beets on the trivet.
2. Lock the lid and set the Pressure Release to Sealing. Select the Pressure Cook or Manual setting and set the cooking time to 10 minutes at high pressure.
3. Once the timer goes off, use a kitchen towel or oven mitts to protect your hand and move the Pressure Release knob to Venting to perform a quick pressure release.
4. Remove the beets, allow to cool, and peel. The skin should slip off easily. Slice the beets into rounds or chop them into bite-sized pieces. Dress them with the balsamic vinegar, olive oil, and salt and pepper to taste.
5. Serve immediately or allow to marinate for 30 minutes for more flavor.

**Nutrition information:**
Calories: 202
Fat: 15 g
Carbs: 3 g
Protein: 12 g

# Garlicky Mashed Sweet Potatoes

(Total Time: 13 Min | Serves: 4)

**Ingredients**
- 4 medium sweet potatoes, peeled and cut into 1-inch chunks
- 1 cup vegetable broth
- 6 cloves garlic, peeled and halved
- ½ cup unsweetened original almond milk
- ½ tablespoon garlic powder
- 3 tablespoons ghee
- Salt to taste
- Pepper to taste
- Optional: 1 tablespoon chopped parsley for serving

**Instructions:**
1. In the Instant Pot, add the sweet potatoes, broth, and garlic. Lock the lid and set the Pressure Release to Sealing. Select the Pressure Cook or Manual setting and set the cooking time to 8 minutes at high pressure.
2. Once the timer goes off, use a kitchen towel or oven mitts to protect your hand and move the Pressure Release knob to Venting to perform a quick pressure release.
3. Open the Instant Pot and mash the potatoes using a potato masher, immersion blender, or fork. Stir in the almond milk, garlic powder, and ghee, and add salt and pepper to taste.
4. Serve warm and sprinkle with fresh parsley, if desired.

**Nutrition information:**
Calories: 200
Fat: 39 g
Carbs: 2 g

Protein: 16 g

# Easiest Baked Sweet Potatoes

(Total Time: 21 Min | Serves: 4)

**Ingredients:**
- 4 medium sweet potatoes

**Instructions:**
1. Place the Instant Pot trivet inside the pot. Prick the potatoes all over with a fork to allow them to vent. Arrange potatoes in one layer on top of the trivet and add 1 cup of water to the pot.
2. Lock the lid and set the Pressure Release to Sealing. Select the Steam setting and set the cooking time to 20 minutes at high pressure.
3. Once the timer goes off, let sit for at least 10 minutes; the pressure will release naturally. Then switch the Pressure Release to Venting to allow any last steam out.
4. Carefully remove the hot potatoes and serve warm.

**Nutrition information:**
Calories: 195
Fat: 19 g
Carbs: 3 g
Protein: 3 g

# Herb Roasted Whole Chicken

(Total Time: 35 Min | Serves: 3)

**Ingredients:**
- 8 lb pastured whole chicken
- ¼ teaspoon sea salt
- ¼ teaspoon black pepper
- ¼ teaspoon rosemary
- ¼ teaspoon thyme
- ¼ teaspoon oregano
- ½ cup pastured butter, diced
- 1 garlic bulb
- 1 orange, sliced
- ½ lemon, sliced

**Instructions:**
1. Take the whole chicken, season it with salt and fill in it with garlic bulb, orange slices and lemon slices; set aside.
2. Next, turn on the Sauté mode of the electric pressure cooker and put in some butter; add in the chicken and keep on changing its side for 2 minutes.
3. Add in the spices along with some water and pressure cook it for 21 minutes.
4. Meanwhile preheat the oven at 370-degree Fahrenheit.
5. After the timer goes off, depressurize the electric cooker naturally and open the lid.
6. Put the chicken in the baking tray along with the left-over juices and place it in the oven for 15 minutes; just grill.
7. Serve the chicken in a serving platter along with baked sweet potatoes.

**Nutrition information:**

Calories 463
Fat 18.8 g
Carbs 27.9 g
Protein 43.4 g

# Tacos With Ham

(Total Time: 30 Min | Serves: 5)

**Ingredients:**
- 2 tablespoons olive oil
- 1 lb cabbage, thinly shredded
- 8 oz Ham slices, browned and crispy, crumbled
- 4 green onions, chopped
- 2 tablespoons chili sauce
- 4 tablespoons sour cream
- ¼ cup onion
- ½ cup roma tomatoes, diced
- ¼ cup cilantro, chopped
- ¼ cup water
- 1 teaspoon salt
- 8 cassava flour taco shells
- 1 avocado, peeled and sliced
- 1 cup goat cheddar cheese, shredded

**Instructions:**
1. Heat olive oil; add onions, tomatoes, cilantro, and salt.
2. Lock the lid and pressure cook this for 6 minutes on high pressure.
3. Unlock and remove the mixture in a bowl.
4. Take one taco shell, place spoonful of onion mixture cooked in pressure cooker, 2 tablespoons crumbled Ham, chili sauce, 2 teaspoons avocado slices, 2 teaspoons sour cream, some shredded cabbage and chopped green onions and top them with shredded cheddar cheese.

**Nutrition information:**
Calories 586
Fat 32 g

Carbs 54.7 g
Protein 22.8 g

# Fettuccine Alfredo

(Total Time: 1 Hour | Serves: 10)

**Ingredients:**
- 1 teaspoon sea salt
- 1 teaspoon black pepper
- 5 packs shirataki fettuccine noodles
- 10 ounces shiitake mushrooms, sliced
- 2 bunches asparagus, trimmed and cut into 2-inch pieces
- 8 tablespoons Italian butter, salted
- 2 cans coconut cream, unsweetened
- 3 cups Parmigiano-Reggiano, grated
- 1 cup parsley, fresh, chopped
- 1 teaspoon Italian seasoning
- 1 lemon, zest only
- 2 cups water
- 1 lb pasteurized chicken, cut into small cubes

**Instructions:**
1. In an electric pressure cooker select the Sauté mode and add in the butter and chicken and cook it for 2 minutes.
2. Now, add in the mushrooms and stir in for 2 minutes.
3. Next, put in the asparagus and stir for 2 minutes.
4. Now, add in the coconut cream and parmigiana into the sauce along with lemon zest, parsley, Italian seasoning and give it a good whisk.
5. Finally add in the fettuccine noodles along with 2 cups of water and close the lid of the pressure cooker.
6. Allow the noodles to get pressured cook for 14 minutes on manual.
7. After the timer goes off, quick release the pressure naturally and open the lid.

8. Finally select the "slow mode" till the Alfredo is fully cooked and the sauce has thickened.
9. Serve the yummy pasta over a serving dish and enjoy while it's hot!

**Nutrition information:**
Calories 478
Fat 15.6 g
Carbs 49.2 g
Protein 37.2 g

# Simplest Brothy Beans

(Total Time: 40 Min | Serves: 4)

**Ingredients:**
- 1 lb. dried white beans, such as great northern, cannellini, or chickpeas
- 1 yellow onion, quartered
- 2 celery stalks, cut in half
- 2 carrots, peeled and cut in half
- 8 cups water
- Salt to taste
- Freshly ground pepper to taste
- Extra virgin olive oil to taste
- Optional: 1 lemon, juiced

**Instructions:**
1. In the Instant Pot, add the beans, onion, celery, carrots, water, and 1 teaspoon of salt. Lock the lid and set the Pressure Release to Sealing. Select the Pressure Cook or Manual setting and set the cooking time to 35 minutes at high pressure.
2. Once the timer goes off, let sit for at least 10 minutes; the pressure will release naturally. Then switch the Pressure Release to Venting to allow any last steam out.
3. Open the Instant Pot and season beans generously with salt and pepper, tasting the broth as you add seasoning until it's to your taste. Serve warm, drizzled with olive oil, and if desired, a squeeze of fresh lemon juice.

**Nutrition information:**
Calories: 285
Fat: 12 g

Carbs: 7 g
Protein: 27 g

# Chicken Tortellini

(Total Time: 35 Min | Serves: 8)

**Ingredients:**
- 3 slices bacon
- ¼ cup + 3 tablespoons grass fed butter
- 4 shallots, peeled and diced
- 1 tablespoon parsley, fresh
- 1 ½ kg pasteurized chicken breasts, boneless
- 1 small carrot, diced
- 1 (8 oz) package dried cheese tortellini
- 1 teaspoon tarragon leaves
- 2 cups rooster broth
- 1 lb asparagus
- 2 tablespoons all-purpose flour
- ¼ cup coconut milk
- ¼ cup heavy cream
- ½ cup hard goat cheese
- ½ teaspoon salt
- ½ teaspoon pepper, seasoning purpose

**Instructions:**
1. Fry the bacon till crisp and keep aside.
2. Stir in butter, shallots, parsley and Sauté for 5 minutes.
3. Reduce the chicken into bite sized chunk pieces; add carrot, tortellini, tarragon and broth. Stir well.
4. Cook this on high pressure for 6 minutes.
5. Do a quick pressure release and add 3 tablespoons butter mixed with flour to the cooker pot.
6. Whisk in milk and cream to the cooker pot, stir the cheese at the end, and cook this till the sauce is thickened.

7. Season with salt and pepper and serve hot.

**Nutrition information:**
Calories 468
Fat 30.5 g
Total Carbs 22.8 g
Protein 26.9 g

# Chicken Cease

(Total Time: 40 Min | Serves: 6)

**Ingredients:**
- 2 tablespoons olive oil
- 2 kg pasteurized chicken breasts, boneless, skinless
- 1 cup chicken broth
- ½ cup Caesar salad dressing
- 4 cloves garlic, minced
- 1 tablespoon Italian seasoning, dried
- 1 cup broccoli florets, frozen, diced
- 1 cup cauliflower florets, diced
- 1 cup frozen carrots, peeled and diced
- ½ cup pimento stuffed olives, sliced
- ½ cup Parmigiano-Reggiano goat cheese

**Instructions:**
- Heat olive oil in a pressure cooker pot and add chunk sized chicken pieces.
- Add in broth, salad dressing, garlic and Italian seasoning mix and stir.
- Lock the lid and cook for 8 minutes.
- Open the pressure cooker pot, add all the other remaining ingredients and cook on high pressure for 2 minutes.
- Garnish with cheese before serving.

**Nutrition information:**
Calories 337
Fat 24.7 g
Total Carbs 10.2 g
Protein 19.9 g

# Chicken And Spinach Quiche

(Total Time: 30 Min | Serves: 6)

**Ingredients:**
- 12 large pasture eggs
- ½ cup coconut milk
- ½ teaspoon sea salt
- ¼ teaspoon ground pepper
- 3 cups fresh baby spinach, roughly chopped
- 1 cup pasteurized chicken pieces, chopped, diced
- 3 large green onions, sliced
- 4 green onion slices, topping the quiche
- ¼ cup goat cheese, shredded

**Instructions:**
1. In a large mixing bowl, whisk eggs, milk, salt, pepper.
2. Add onions, chicken pieces, chopped spinach leaves in a baking quiche mound. Pour the egg mixture from the top.
3. Garnish with green onion slices and grated goat cheese.
4. In an electric cooker pot, add 1½ cup water and put a steamer rack in it.
5. Next, place the quiche mound on the rack or the metal trivet.
6. Lock the cooker lid and cook on high pressure for 20 minutes. Leave it aside for 10 minutes.
7. Do a pressure release and remove the quiche and serve hot.

**Nutrition information:**
Calories 249
Fat 15.3 g
Carbs 4.7 g
Protein 23.2 g

# Quail Tortellini

(Total Time: 30 Min | Serves: 6)

**Ingredients:**
- 3 slices bacon
- 3 tablespoons butter
- 4 shallots, peeled and diced
- 1 tablespoon parsley, fresh
- 1½ kg pasteurized quail breasts, boneless
- 1 small carrot, diced
- 1 8 oz cheese tortellini, dried
- 1 teaspoon tarragon leaves
- 2 cups pasteurized chicken broth
- 1 lb asparagus
- 2 tablespoons all-purpose flour
- ¼ cup coconut milk
- ¼ cup coconut cream
- ½ cup goat cheese
- ½ teaspoon salt
- ½ teaspoon pepper

**Instructions:**
1. Fry the bacon till crisp and keep aside.
2. Stir in butter, shallots, parsley and sauté for 5 minutes.
3. Reduce the quail into bite sized chunk pieces; add carrot, tortellini, tarragon and broth. Stir well.
4. Cook this on high pressure for 6 minutes.
5. Do a quick pressure release and add 3 tablespoons butter mixed with flour to the cooker pot.
6. Whisk in milk and cream to the cooker pot, stir the cheese at the end, and cook this till the sauce is thickened.
7. Season with salt and pepper and serve hot.

**Nutrition information:**
Calories 1208
Fat 44.2 g
Carbs 53.7 g
Protein 146.2 g

# Beef Stroganoff With Miracle Noodles

(Total Time: 40 Min | Serves: 6)

## Ingredients:
- 2 lb grass fed pork
- ¼ teaspoon sea salt
- ¼ teaspoon pepper, freshly grounded
- 1 tablespoon olive oil
- 1 medium onion
- 1 cup dry white wine
- 1 tablespoon Dijon mustard
- 1 cup pasture chicken broth, low salt
- 1 tablespoon cassava flour
- 1 lb Portobello mushrooms
- 3 carrots
- 2 stalks celery
- ¼ cup goat cheddar cheese
- ¼ cup parsley, freshly chopped
- 12 oz miracle noodles

## Instructions:
1. Toss the pork pieces with half teaspoon sea salt and pepper.
2. Heat oil in the pressure cooker, add the pork and cook stirring occasionally till sides are browned.
3. Add the onions, cook till soft, and now add dry white wine, mustard, flour. Bring this to simmer and cook till reduced half.
4. Add the chicken broth, celery, carrots and mushrooms.
5. Close the lid and bring to high pressure over medium heat and cook till 18 minutes.
6. Remove from heat using quick release method.
7. Stir in the cheese, parsley and remaining salt and pepper to taste.

8. Cook miracle noodles as per the instructions on the packet. Mix well in the pork stroganoff and serve.

**Nutrition information:**
Calories 376
Fat 16.2 g
Carbs 22.1 g
Protein 28.2g

# Burrito With Pork

(Total Time: 30 Min | Serves: 6)

## Ingredients:
- 2 tablespoons olive oil
- 8 oz pork pieces, browned and chopped
- 8 oz miracle rice, cooked
- ¼ cup onion
- ½ cup diced roma tomatoes
- ¼ cup cilantro, chopped
- ¼ cup water
- 1 teaspoon salt
- 4 giant cassava flour tortillas
- 1 avocado, peeled and sliced
- Goat cheddar cheese, shredded

## Instructions:
1. Heat olive oil; add pork pieces and stir fry till nicely browned. Add Miracle rice and mix together well. Remove and keep aside.
2. Add onions, tomatoes, cilantro and salt.
3. Lock the lid and pressure cook this for 6 minutes.
4. Unlock and remove the mixture in a bowl. Mix the rice and tofu mixture well.
5. Take one tortilla sheet, place spoonful of pork and rice mixture cooked in pressure cooker, 2 tablespoons of onion mixture, some avocado slices, shredded cheddar cheese and roll them tightly.
6. Cut them into small bites and serve with choice of sauce.

## Nutrition information:
Calories 114
Fat 7.9 g

Carbs 8.6 g
Protein 3.2 g

# Meat Lovers Quiche

(Total Time: 40 Min | Serves: 6)

### Ingredients:
- 6 large pastured eggs
- ½ cup coconut milk
- ¼ teaspoon sea salt
- 1/8 teaspoon ground pepper
- 4 slices bacon, cooked and crumbled
- ½ cup ham, chopped
- ½ cup goat cheddar cheese, shredded

### Instructions:
1. In a large mixing bowl, whisk eggs, milk, salt, pepper.
2. Add all the dry ingredients in a baking quiche mound. Pour the egg mixture from the top.
3. Garnish with crumbled bacon and grated cheddar cheese.
4. In a cooker pot, add 1 ½ cup water and place the rack. Place the quiche mound on the rack or the metal trivet.
5. Lock the cooker lid and cook on high pressure for 20 minutes. Leave it aside for 10 minutes.
6. Do a pressure release and remove the quiche and serve hot.

### Nutrition information:
Calories 235
Fat 18 g
Carbs 2.9 g
Protein 15.2 g

# Beef Inventory

(Total Time: 40 Min | Serves: 6)

**Ingredients:**
- 3 lb lean beef
- ½ lb carrots, chopped
- ½ lb onions, chopped
- ½ lb celery, chopped
- 1 tablespoon kosher salt
- ½ teaspoon black peppercorns
- Water

**Instructions:**
1. Mix all the ingredients in the pressure cooker pot along with water.
2. Add sufficient water to cover all the ingredients.
3. Cook on high pressure for 20 minutes.
4. Do a natural pressure release and strain this inventory using cheesecloth.

**Nutrition information:**
Calories 458
Fat 14.2 g
Carbs 8.5 g
Protein 69.8 g

# Braised Pork With Italian Seasoning

(Total Time: 50 Min | Serves: 7)

**Ingredients:**
- 3 lb grass fed pork loin, roasted
- 2 tablespoons olive oil
- 1 tablespoon Italian seasoning
- ¼ teaspoon salt
- ¼ teaspoon pepper

**Instructions:**
1. Rub the pork with salt, pepper and Italian seasoning.
2. Heat the olive oil and add the pork, cook till evenly browned.
3. Pour 1½ cups water and shut the lid. Cook for 25 minutes on high pressure.
4. Do a natural pressure release and then open the lid slowly.
5. Let the pork be relaxed for 5 minutes before slicing. Serve hot!

**Nutrition information:**
Calories 511
Fat 31.7 g
Carbs 0.3 g
Protein 53.1 g

# Tacos With Bacon

(Total Time: 30 Min | Serves: 5)

**Ingredients:**
- 2 tablespoons olive oil
- 1 lb cabbage, thinly shredded
- 8 oz bacon slices, browned and crispy, crumbled
- 4 green onions, chopped
- 2 tablespoons chili sauce
- 4 tablespoons sour cream
- ¼ cup onion
- ½ cup roma tomatoes, diced
- ¼ cup cilantro, chopped
- ¼ cup water
- 1 teaspoon salt
- 8 taco shells
- 1 avocado, peeled and sliced
- 1 cup goat cheddar cheese, shredded

**Instructions:**
1. Heat olive oil; add onions, tomatoes, cilantro, and salt.
2. Lock the lid and pressure cook this for 6 minutes on high pressure.
3. Unlock and remove the mixture in a bowl.
4. Take one taco shell, place spoonful of onion mixture cooked in pressure cooker, 2 tablespoons crumbled bacon, chili sauce, 2 teaspoons avocado slices, 2 teaspoons sour cream, some shredded cabbage and chopped green onions and top them with shredded cheddar cheese and sour cream.

**Nutrition information:**
Calories 394
Fat 25.1 g

Carbs 29.3 g
Protein 13.4 g

# Stuffed Bacon In Artichoke

(Total Time: 40 Min | Serves: 4)

**Ingredients:**
- 8 artichokes, medium sized
- 1 cup water
- 6 slices bacon, crumbled and cooked
- 1 cup goat cheese, crumbled
- 2 teaspoons salt
- 1 teaspoon pepper
- ½ teaspoon nutmeg powder
- 2 cups bread crumbs, lectin free
- 2 large pastured eggs
- 2 tablespoons olive oil

**Instructions:**
1. Clean and trim the artichokes well.
2. Place them upside down for opening and creating a hole or dent in the center.
3. In a mixing bowl, place all the above-mentioned ingredients and reserve half the cheese for using a topping. Lastly mix crumbled bacon to the mixture.
4. Take the artichokes and fill them well with this filling.
5. Garnish with the remaining half cheese.
6. Place the stuffed artichokes on the rack or the metal trivet. Cook this on high pressure for 5 to 7 minutes.
7. Do a quick pressure release and remove the stuffed artichokes on a serving platter.

**Nutrition information:**
Calories 100
Fat 2 g

Carbs 18 g
Protein 3 g

## Lamb With Portobello Mushrooms

(Total Time: 40 Min | Serves: 6)

**Ingredients:**
- 2 lb grass-fed lamb chops
- 3 cans Portobello mushrooms
- 1 lb baby carrots
- 2 cups water
- 1 pack miracle noodles, cooked and buttered
- ¼ teaspoon salt
- ¼ teaspoon pepper

**Instructions:**
1. Put the mushrooms in the pressure cooker pot.
2. Add water and stir well to combine.
3. Stir carrots and place the lamb chops in the pressure cooker.
4. Sprinkle with a touch of seasoning over it.
5. Lock the pressure cooker lid and cook this on high pressure for 20 minutes.
6. Release pressure and first serve the lamb chops, top them with carrots and the sauce from the cooker pot.

**Nutrition information:**
Calories 287
Fat 9.9 g
Carbs 8.1 g
Protein 39.6 g

# Ham Filled Egg Muffins

(Total Time: 30 Min | Serves: 6)

**Ingredients:**
- 4 pastured eggs
- ¼ teaspoon lemon pepper seasoning
- 4 tablespoons goat cheddar cheese, shredded
- 1 green onion, diced
- 4 slices grass-fed ham, precooked

**Instructions:**
1. Add 1½ cups water and place the rack in the cooker pot.
2. In a mixing bowl, break eggs and whisk well. Add all the other ingredients and divide the muffin batter equally in muffin mounds.
3. Place these muffins on the rack or metal trivet. Cook this on high pressure on 8 minutes.
4. Do a natural pressure release and remove the cooked muffins carefully.

**Nutrition information:**
Calories 163
Fat 11.3 g
Carbs 2.1 g
Protein 12.9 g

# Cabbage Rolls With Pork

(Total Time: 55 Min | Serves: 6)

**Ingredients:**
- 1 cup miracle rice
- 1 large head cabbage
- 1 large pastured egg
- 1 cup onion, chopped
- 4 garlic cloves, minced and pasted
- ½ teaspoon salt
- ½ teaspoon pepper powder
- 1½ lb grass fed lean pork, grounded

For sauce:
- 2 tablespoons grass fed butter
- 1 cup onions, finely chopped
- 3 garlic cloves, minced
- 28 Oz roma tomatoes, blanched, peeled and deseed
- ¼ cup white vinegar
- 2 teaspoons low sodium grass fed instant beef bouillon
- ½ teaspoon garlic powder
- ½ teaspoon onion powder
- ½ teaspoon pepper powder
- 4 dashes Worcestershire sauce
- 2 tablespoons cold water
- ½ cup parsley, freshly chopped
- 4 tablespoons tapioca flour
- ½ cup tomato sauce

**Instructions:**

For the sauce:
1. Melt butter in a saucepan, add onion and garlic and all the other ingredients mentioned above required to make sauce.

For the cabbage rolls:
1. Cook the rice according to the packet and keep aside.
2. Fill a large deep pot half full of water. Bring to boil and add the large head cabbage for 7-8 minutes.
3. Remove the softened leaves and keep aside. Keep this process repeating till all the leaves are softened and tender.
4. Cook the remaining cabbage well and chop into pieces and keep aside.
5. In a large bowl, beat the egg, stir in onion, garlic, salt, pepper and cooked rice. Add ground pork and combine all ingredients well.
6. Lay one cabbage leaf; place 2 tbsp. of filling on it. Roll the cabbage well and keep aside. Toothpick can be used to secure rolls.
7. Now place the rack in the cooker pot. Pour 1 cup water. Place 7-8 rolls on the rack. Cover the rolls with about 1/3 of the sauce. Repeat another layer of rolls over the previous one.
8. Lock the lid and cook on high pressure for 18 minutes. Do a quick pressure release and unlock the lid.
9. Remove the rolls carefully and reduce the sauce in the pressure cooker pot till thick.
10. Serve the cabbage rolls with sauce poured on top.

**Nutrition information:**
Calories 377
Fat 19.5 g
Carbs 12.9 g
Protein 34.7 g

# Braised Pork With Marinara Sauce

(Total Time: 50 Min | Serves: 7)

## Ingredients:
- 3 lb grass-fed pork loin roast
- 2 tablespoons olive oil
- 1 tablespoon Italian seasoning
- 1 cup marinara sauce
- ¼ teaspoon salt
- ¼ teaspoon pepper

## Instructions
1. Rub the pork with salt, pepper and Italian seasoning.
2. Heat the olive oil and add the pork, cook till evenly browned.
3. Pour 1½ cups water and shut the lid. Cook for 25 minutes on high pressure.
4. Do a natural pressure release and then open the lid slowly.
5. Add the marinara sauce and let the pork coat the sauce well.
6. Let the pork be relaxed for 5 minutes before slicing. Serve hot topped with marinara sauce from the cooker pot.

## Nutrition information:
Calories 350
Fat 12.4 g
Carbs 5.2 g
Protein 51.5 g

# Fiery Bbq Meat Balls

(Total Time: 30 Min | Serves: 8)

**Ingredients:**
- 1 bag (48 oz.) beef meatballs, frozen fully cooked, grass fed beef
- 18 oz BBQ sauce
- 3-4 tablespoons Habanero Pepper Jelly
- 3 oz beef stock, grass fed beef

**Instructions:**
1. Add 1 cup water in pressure cooker
2. Add frozen meatballs to the steamer basket and pressure cook for 5 minutes on high.
3. When beeps, do a quick pressure release and remove the meatballs from electric cooker pot.
4. Discard cooking water and add BBQ sauce, beef broth and habanero pepper jelly to pressure cooker.
5. Select Sauté; cook till the sauce is smooth.
6. Add heated meatballs and stir to combine.
7. Serve hot. Keep them warm until serving.

**Nutrition information:**
Calories 146
Fat 3 g
Carbs 23.1 g
Protein 5.9 g

# Lamb Empanadas

(Total Time: 1Hour 35 Min|Serves: 6)

**Ingredients:**
- ½ cup red onion, diced
- 4 garlic cloves, chopped
- ½ poblano pepper, diced
- ½ cup fresh cilantro, chopped
- 3 lbs grass fed lamb meat, grounded
- 3 teaspoons Himalayan salt
- 4 teaspoons garlic powder
- 2 teaspoons black pepper, grounded
- 1 teaspoon oregano
- 2 teaspoons onion powder
- 14.5 oz roma tomatoes, blanched, peeled, deseeded and diced
- 10 Oz. goat cheddar cheese
- 6 almond flour empanadas
- 2 tablespoons grass-fed butter
- 1 large pastured egg, whisked for egg wash

**Instructions:**
1. Put some butter in the electric pressure cooker and add in the lamb, salt, garlic powder, black pepper, oregano, onion powder and mix; add in 2 cups of water and pressure cook lamb mince for 20 minutes.
2. After the timer goes off, depressurize the cooker naturally and open the lid carefully. Dry the water if any.
3. Preheat the oven at 400 degree Fahrenheit.
4. Next, select Sauté mode and add in the onions and garlic cloves along with the lamb mince and give it a good mix for 10 minutes.
5. Now, add in the tomatoes and keep on mixing it for 10 minutes.

6. After that, add in the poblano pepper and keep on mixing it for 5 minutes.
7. Transfer the mixture onto a plate.
8. Fill each empanada with the mixture and fold it into semicircles and prick it from ends.
9. Coat each empanada with the egg wash and place them on a greased baking sheet.
10. Bake the empanadas for 10-15 minutes.
11. Take them out from the oven and serve it on a platter.
12. Enjoy eating!

**Nutrition information:**
Calories 507
Fat 4.1 g
Carbs 2.2 g
Protein 3.7 g

# Pork With Risotto

(Total Time: 45 Min | Serves: 8)

**Ingredients:**
- 6 bones in grass-fed pork chops
- 2 tablespoons grass-fed butter
- 1 cup miracle rice, dried
- 1 onion, chopped
- ½ cup red wine
- 1 tablespoon garlic, minced
- 1 lemon juice, zest
- 1½ cups grass-fed rooster broth
- 1/3 cup goat parmesan cheese

**Instructions:**
1. Warm the butter and add the pork chops and cook till nicely browned.
2. Stir within garlic and onion and cook dinner till softened, about 3 minutes.
3. Add the miracle rice and let it coat butter well.
4. Add red wine, lemon juice and zest to the miracle rice in the cooker pot.
5. Shut the cooker lid and cook on high pressure for 20 minutes.
6. Do a quick pressure release method.
7. Stir in goat parmesan cheese well and serve immediately.

**Nutrition information:**
Calories 197
Fat 8.5 g
Carbs 2.7 g
Protein 23 g

# Chapter 8: Snacks

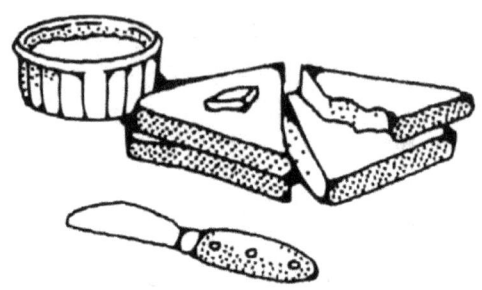

## Pressure Cooked Onion With Herbed Butter

(Total Time: 20 Min|Serves: 6)

**Ingredients:**
- 3 large onion bulbs
- 1 cup water
- Herb butter, for rubbing onion

**Instructions:**
1. Slice off ¼ of the onion bulb from the top keeping the bulb intact.
2. Prepare the pressure cooker pot by adding water and place the rack on it.
3. Keep the onion bulb on the rack and pressure cook for 5-6 minutes on high pressure.

4. Do a natural pressure release and remove the soft onion very carefully.
5. Keep this onion bulb on a grill rack in the oven for 5 minutes to get crispy browned onion bulb.

**Nutrition information:**
Calories 14
Fat 0.5 g
Carbs 1.9 g
Protein 0.9g

# Pressure Cooker Polenta

(Total Time: 15 Min | Serves: 6)

**Ingredients:**
- 2 cups polenta, coarse
- 8 cups water
- 2 teaspoons salt

**Instructions:**
1. Fill the electric pressure cooker with the water and bring this water to a boil.
2. Add salt and polenta flour to the boiling water.
3. Keep stirring this continuously and close the lid of the cooker pot.
4. Cook this on high pressure for 8 minutes.
5. Do a natural pressure release and check the consistency of the polenta.

**Nutrition information:**
Calories 185
Fat 0.5 g
Carbs 40.6 g
Protein 3.8g

# Steamed Sweet Potatoes

(Total Time: 20 Min|Serves: 6)

**Ingredients:**
- 10 baby sweet potatoes
- 1½ cup water

**Instructions:**
1. Place 1½ cups water in the cooker pot and place the rack or metal trivet.
2. Wash and keep the sweet baby potatoes on the steamer rack.
3. Lock the lid and cook this on high pressure for 8-10 minutes.
4. Do a pressure release and remove the baby potatoes carefully.
5. Season with salt and pepper. For crispier potatoes place them in the oven on grill rack for 5 minutes.

**Nutrition information:**
Calories 83
Fat 0 g
Carbs 18.3 g
Protein 1.7 g

# Caramelized Onion

(Total Time: 20 Min | Serves: 4)

**Ingredients:**
- 3 large onion bulbs
- 1 cup water

**Instructions:**
1. Slice off ¼ of the onion bulb from the top, keeping the bulb intact.
2. Prepare the pressure cooker pot by adding water and place the rack on it.
3. Keep the onion bulb on the rack and pressure cook for 5-6 minutes on high pressure.
4. Do a natural pressure release and remove the soft onion very carefully.
5. Keep this onion bulb on a grill rack in the oven for 5 minutes to get crispy browned onion bulb.

**Nutrition information:**
Calories 6
Fat 0 g
Carbs 1.4 g
Protein 0.2 g

# Roasted Whole Garlic

(Total Time: 25 Min|Serves: 6)

**Ingredients:**
- 3 large garlic bulbs.
- 1 cup water

**Instructions:**
1. Slice off ¼ of the garlic bulb form the top keeping the bulb intact.
2. Prepare the pressure cooker pot by adding water and place the rack on it.
3. Keep the garlic bulb on the rack and pressure cook for 5-6 minutes on high pressure.
4. Do a natural pressure release and remove the soft garlic very carefully.
5. Keep this in on a grill rack in the oven for 5 minutes to get crispy garlic bulb.

**Nutrition information:**
Calories 8
Fat 0 g
Carbs 1.5 g
Protein 0 g

# Roasted Whole Garlic With Herded Butter

(Total Time: 25 Min | Serves: 6)

**Ingredients:**
- 3 large garlic bulbs
- 1 cup water
- 1 tablespoons herbed butter

**Instructions:**
1. Slice off ¼ of the garlic bulb from the top keeping the bulb intact.
2. Prepare the pressure cooker pot by adding water and place the rack on it.
3. Keep the garlic bulb on the rack and pressure cook for 5-6 minutes on high pressure.
4. Do a natural pressure release and remove the soft garlic very carefully. Apply the herbed butter on the garlic bulb.
5. Keep this in on a grill rack in the oven for 5 minutes to get crispy garlic bulb.

**Nutrition information:**
Calories 28
Fat 1.5 g
Carbs 1.7 g
Protein 1.4 g

# Chapter 9: Soups And Salads

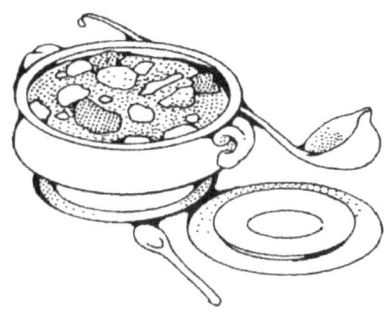

## Easy Noodle Soup

(Total Time: 40 Min|Serves: 4)

**Ingredients:**
- ¼ cup sesame oil
- 1 onion, julienned
- 2 teaspoons ginger, julienned
- 2 cans Portobello mushrooms, sliced
- 4 baby bok choy, thinly sliced
- 4 cups vegetable stock
- 12 oz raw shrimps
- 1 packet miracle noodles, boiled and rinsed
- 3 tablespoons coconut amino
- 5-6 lemon wedges

**Instructions:**
1. In an electric pressure cooker add in some oil and put in chopped onions; select the Sauté mode and allow it to cook for 5 minutes.

2. Next put ginger, mushrooms and bok choy in it and give it a good mix for 2 minutes.
3. Now, add in the vegetable broth and shrimps in it, and cover the electric cooker with the lid; allow it to cook for 20 minutes on soup mode.
4. After the timer goes off, quick release the pressure naturally and pen the lid.
5. Now, add in the miracle noodles and let it cook for another 2 minutes.
6. Transfer the soup in the serving bowl and enjoy eating while serving it with lemon wedges.

**Nutrition information:**
Calories 512
Fat 30.6 g
Carbs 16 g
Protein 43.9 g

# Caesar Salads

(Total Time: 1Hour 40 Min | Serves: 8)

**Ingredients:**
- 12 drops of liquid stevia
- 2 cod fillets
- ½ teaspoon salt
- 2 romaine lettuce, large heads, rinsed thoroughly
- 4 cloves garlic, small, minced
- ¾ cup extra virgin olive oil
- 2 teaspoon Dijon mustard
- 1 ½ cup garbanzo beans
- 4 tablespoons lemon juice
- 4 tablespoons nutritional yeast

**Instructions:**
1. Season the cod with salt and set aside.
2. Next, take the electric pressure cooker and place a trivet inside it.
3. Place the cod over the steamer rack and pressure cook it for 15 minutes.
4. After the timer goes off, quick release the pressure naturally and open the lid.
5. Transfer the cod onto the plate and set aside.
6. Put the garbanzo beans in a pressure cooker along with 2 cups of water and pressure cook it for 15 minutes on medium-high pressure.
7. After the timer goes off, release the pressure naturally then open the lid.
8. Next strain the beans and set aside.
9. Take a food blender and mix in the beans, garlic, olive oil, lemon, mustard and yeast, stevia, salt, and lemon juice in a food processor and blend until smooth.

10. Transfer the dressing in an air tight container and let it sit in the refrigerator for about 1 hour.
11. Now take all the lettuce in a large bowl and cover it with the dressing and toss for a minute until the dressing is evenly distributed.
12. Serve the salad in a serving dish and enjoy eating.

**Nutrition information:**
Calories 346
Fat 21.8 g
Carbs 26.3 g
Protein 14.9 g

# Cauliflower Soup

(Total Time: 30 Min | Serves: 6)

## Ingredients:
- 2 tablespoons extra virgin olive oil
- 1 onion, chopped
- 2 teaspoons ginger, freshly chopped
- 2 garlic cloves, chopped
- 2 bunch cauliflower, florets only
- 2 teaspoons curry powder
- 1 teaspoon cumin
- ½ teaspoon salt
- 2 cups coconut milk
- 6 cups vegetable stock
- Few leaves coriander
- 4 almonds, blanched and sliced

## Instructions:
1. Put olive oil in the pressure cooker and add in the onions while selecting the sauté mode in it, for 2-3 minutes.
2. Next add in the garlic cloves, ginger and cauliflower florets and allow it to Sauté for 4 minutes.
3. Add in the spices such as cumin and salt.
4. Next, add in the almond milk along with vegetable stock and pressure cook it for 10 minutes by selecting the soup mode.
5. After the timer goes off, press cancel and quick release the pressure naturally and open the lid.
6. Puree the soup until it gets a smooth consistency.
7. Transfer the soup into the serving bowls topped up with coriander leaves and blanched almonds.
8. Enjoy eating.

## Nutrition information:

Calories 260
Fat 24.5 g
Carbs 10.1 g
Protein 3.9 g

# Asparagus Salad

(Total Time: 30 Min | Serves: 4)

### Ingredients:
- 1 lemon juice
- 2 salmon fillets
- 1 tablespoon champagne vinegar
- 1 tablespoons walnut oil
- 1 tablespoon Dijon mustard
- ¼ cup goat parmesan cheese, shredded
- ¼ cup fresh mint
- ¼ cup pine nuts, roasted
- ¼ teaspoon pepper
- 2 cups asparagus, shaved

### Instructions:
1. Season the salmon with salt and set aside.
2. Next, take the electric pressure cooker and place a trivet inside it.
3. Place the salmon over the steamer rack and pressure cook it for 15 minutes.
4. After the timer goes off, quick release the pressure naturally and open the lid.
5. Transfer the salmon onto the plate and set aside.
6. In a serving plate put all the salmon and the asparagus and set aside.
7. In a small bowl put some lemon juice along with walnut oil, mustard, champagne vinegar, and give it a good whisk.
8. Drizzle the dressing over the raw asparagus and garnish it with pine nuts, pepper, mint and cheddar cheese.

### Nutrition information:

Calories 323
Fat 21.7 g
Carbs 5.5 g
Protein 28.5 g

# Smoked Paprika Lentil Soup

(Total Time: 35 Min | Serves: 6)

### Ingredients:
- 1 cup red lentils, rinsed, skinless
- 1 cup green/brown lentils, skinless, rinsed
- 1 medium onion, chopped finely
- 3 cloves garlic, minced
- 2 teaspoons cumin
- 1½ teaspoon smoked paprika
- 2 carrots, sliced
- 2 celery stalks
- 1 bunch spinach
- 8 cups water
- 1 teaspoon salt
- 1 teaspoon pepper

### Instructions:
1. Take an electric pressure cooker and select Sauté and add oil, garlic, onion, spices, carrots, and celery for 5 minutes until onion soften.
2. Stir in the lentils and add water to cover.
3. Lock the lid into place and allow it to cook on high pressure for 10 minutes on soup mode and then on sauté mode for 5 minutes.
4. Use quick release method to release the pressure and unlock the lid safely.
5. Add in the smoked paprika, cumin, salt and pepper and serve hot on a serving dish.

### Nutrition information:
Calories 179
Fat 1.2 g

Carbs 31.8 g

# Orzo Soup With Butternut Squash

(Total Time: 35 Min | Serves: 3)

**Ingredients:**
- 3 tablespoons butter
- ½ cup green onions, diced
- ½ cup celery, diced
- ½ carrots, diced
- 1 garlic clove, minced
- 1 (4.5 oz.) can diced roma tomatoes with juice
- ½ teaspoon Italian seasoning
- 1/8 teaspoon red pepper flakes
- ¼ teaspoon pepper, freshly grounded
- 1/8 teaspoon nutmeg, freshly grated
- 1 cup orzo, cooked
- 1½ lb. butternut squash, diced
- 2 tablespoons scallion, thinly sliced for garnish
- 2 cups water
- 1 teaspoon half and half

**Instructions:**
1. Melt butter in the electric pressure cooker and select the Sauté mode while adding in the onions, celery and carrots. Add garlic and stir briefly.
2. Add canned tomatoes and squash. Also add nutmeg, red pepper flakes and Italian seasoning.
3. Select high pressure and cook time of 10 minutes on soup mode.
4. When you hear the beep sound, turn the pressure cooker off. Wait for 10 minutes before opening the lid by doing a Quick pressure release.
5. Puree the mixture until smooth and creamy. Select simmer and add orzo and allow it to cook.

6. Serve with a swirl of half and half and some sprinkled green onion thins.

**Nutrition information:**
Calories 217
Fat 4.2 g
Carbs 43.8 g
Protein 4.9g

# Fall Kale Salad

(Total Time: 30 Min | Serves: 6)

### Ingredients:
- 1 lemon juice
- 2 salmon fillets
- ¼ cup extra virgin oil
- 1 teaspoon Dijon mustard
- I tablespoon red wine vinegar
- 4 cups kale, thinly sliced, ribs removed
- 1 teaspoon salt
- 1 avocado, diced
- 1 cup pomegranate seeds
- 1 cup walnuts, toasted
- 1 cup goat parmesan cheese, shredded

### Instructions:
1. Season the salmon with salt and set aside.
2. Next, take the electric pressure cooker and place a trivet inside it.
3. Place the salmon over the steamer rack and pressure cook it for 15 minutes.
4. After the timer goes off, quick release the pressure naturally and open the lid.
5. Transfer the salmon onto the plate and set aside.
6. In a bowl take some kale and season it with salt; set aside.
7. In another bowl make the dressing for the salad by combining lemon juice with olive oil, Dijon mustard and red wine vinegar.
8. Season kale with the dressing and add in the diced avocado, pomegranate seeds, walnuts and parmesan cheese.
9. Give it a good toss and serve it in a platter.

**Nutrition information:**
Calories 234
Fat 14.3 g
Carbs 12.6 g
Protein 16 g

# Mixed Veggie Soup

(Total Time: 25 Min | Serves: 10)

Ingredients:
- 2 tablespoons olive oil
- 1 carrot, peeled and minced
- 1 celery stalk, minced
- 1 small onion, minced
- 2 garlic cloves, minced
- 1 teaspoon dried sage, crushed
- 1 teaspoon dried rosemary, crushed
- 8-ounce fresh Portabello mushrooms, sliced
- 8-ounce fresh white mushrooms, sliced
- ½ cup red wine
- 2 carrots, peeled and chopped
- 2 sweet potatoes, peeled and chopped
- 1½ cups fresh green beans, trimmed and chopped
- 1 tablespoon balsamic vinegar
- 3 cups water
- 2 tablespoons potato flour
- ¼ cup water
- ½ teaspoon salt
- ½ teaspoon black pepper
- ¾ cup pearl onion

Instructions:
1. Pour the oil in the Instant Pot and select "Sauté".
2. Then add in the carrots, celery and onion and cook for about 2-3 minutes. Add garlic and herbs and cook for about 1 minute.
3. Next, add mushrooms and cook for about 4-5 minutes. Add the wine and cook for about 2 minutes, scraping the brown bits from the bottom.

4. Select "Cancel" and stir in the carrots, potatoes, green beans, vinegar and water. Next, secure the lid and cook under "Manual" and "High Pressure" for about 15 minutes.
5. Select "Cancel" and carefully do a quick release.
6. Meanwhile in a bowl, dissolve potato flour into water.
7. Remove the lid of Instant Pot and immediately, stir in potato flour mixture, salt, black pepper and pearl onion. Select "Sauté" and cook for about 1 minute.
8. Serve hot.

**Nutrition information:**
Calories 124
Fat 3.4 g
Carbs 20.2 g
Protein 4.2 g

# Seed-Sar Salad

(Total Time: 40 Min | Serves: 4)

**Ingredients:**
- 10 oz romaine leaves, washed thoroughly
- 2 salmon fillets
- 2 cups cocktail shrimps, cooked
- 12 oz crab meat
- 1 cup raw pumpkin seeds
- 2 garlic cloves, crushed
- ½ teaspoons sea salt
- ½ teaspoon black pepper, cracked
- 1 lemon juice
- 2 teaspoons Dijon mustard
- ½ cup goat parmesan cheese, shredded
- 8 tablespoons extra-virgin olive oil

**Instructions:**
1. Season the salmon with salt and set aside.
2. Next, take the electric pressure cooker and place a trivet inside it.
3. Place the salmon over the steamer rack and pressure cook it for 15 minutes.
4. After the timer goes off, quick release the pressure naturally and open the lid.
5. Transfer the salmon onto the plate and set aside.
6. In a food processor add in the raw pumpkin seeds, garlic cloves, sea salt, black pepper, and lemon juice, Dijon mustard plus olive oil and blend until a smooth puree is formed.
7. Next, place the romaine leaves on a serving platter and drizzle the dressing over it; mix until all the leaves are coated.

8. Serve it with shrimps and crab meat over the top along with cheese and freshly grounded pepper.

**Nutrition information:**
Calories 732
Fat 34.3 g
Carbs 7.1 g
Protein 27.3 g

# Broccoli Cheddar Soup

(Total Time: 25 Min | Serves: 4)

## Ingredients:
- ¼ cup extra virgin olive oil
- 1 yellow onion, minced
- 2 celery, diced
- 3 cloves garlic, minced
- 1 teaspoon salt
- 1 teaspoon black pepper
- 2 cups broccoli, florets
- 1 cup coconut cream
- 2 cups vegetable broth
- 1 cup goat's milk cheddar cheese

## Instructions:
1. In a pressure cooker put in the olive oil along with yellow onion and Sauté it for 5 minutes.
2. Next, add in the celery ribs, garlic cloves, and salt, pepper and broccoli florets in it and give it a good mix.
3. Now, add in the coconut cream along with vegetable broth.
4. Close the lid of the cooker and pressure cook it for 15 minutes on soup mode.
5. After the timer goes off, quick release the pressure naturally.
6. Now add in the cheddar cheese and cook it for another 1 minute.
7. Transfer it in the serving bowl and enjoy eating.

## Nutrition information:
Calories 322
Fat 29.6 g
Carbs 11.1 g
Protein 7.6 g

www.ingramcontent.com/pod-product-compliance
Lightning Source LLC
Chambersburg PA
CBHW071437070526
44578CB00001B/115